illuminated while waiting

Arise in
the light
of God's
promises

Elizabeth Hughes

Illuminated While Waiting —Copyright ©2025 by Elizabeth A. Hughes
Published by UNITED HOUSE Publishing

All rights reserved. No portion of this book may be reproduced or shared in any form–electronic, printed, photocopied, recording, or by any information storage and retrieval system, without prior written permission from the publisher. The use of short quotations is permitted.

Unless otherwise indicated, all Scripture quotations are taken from:

The Holy Bible, English Standard Version® (ESV®)
Copyright © 2001 by Crossway,
a publishing ministry of Good News Publishers.
All rights reserved.

ESV Text Edition: 2016
The Holy Bible, English Standard Version (ESV) is adapted from the Revised Standard Version of the Bible, copyright Division of Christian Education of the National Council of the Churches of Christ in the U.S.A. All rights reserved.

ISBN: 978-1-952840-71-5

UNITED HOUSE Publishing
Waterford, Michigan
info@unitedhousepublishing.com
www.unitedhousepublishing.com

Interior design:
Matt Russell, In The Light Creative, matt@inthelightcreative.com

Printed in the United States of America
2025—First Edition

SPECIAL SALES
Most UNITED HOUSE books are available at special quantity discounts when purchased in bulk by corporations, organizations, and special-interest groups. For information, please e-mail orders@unitedhousepublishing.com

"*Illuminated While Waiting* is a powerful and timely guide for anyone navigating a season of waiting with God. The author masterfully blends scripture, heartfelt storytelling, and practical wisdom to remind us that delays are not denials—they are divine opportunities for growth and trust. This book is a must-read for those seeking purpose, peace, and God's presence in the waiting. Each page feels like a gentle conversation with a trusted mentor, encouraging you to surrender and trust God's perfect timing. I highly recommend it to anyone looking for encouragement and hope in their faith journey."

—Melissa Mendez
Author of *Restorative Self-Care Planning Journal*

"If you are ready to transform your season of waiting from one of worry and darkness to hope and light, *Illuminated While Waiting* is for you! Whether your season of waiting is long or short, this book will provide you with refreshed encouragement and renewed hope in God's promises. Elizabeth's powerful insights help you to remember that you can laugh along the journey the Lord is leading you, as He guides you to the promises He has spoken with His lantern in hand."

—Hilary Frank
Author of *Marrying Freedom*

"I am truly excited about Elizabeth's book for all those "in waiting". The waiting season is always around another corner. We seem to hit several roadblocks in our lives where God is asking us to wait again! I know this book is going to encourage women in any season of waiting on the promises of God. I'm so thankful for the encouragement to endure the process of the wait that sits in these pages for those who need it!"

—Kendra Dee Carroll
Author of *Step into Your Calling,*
Ministry Makers God's Yes Girls
Podcaster, Speaker, Leadership Development

"This is one woman's authentic testimony of God's overcoming power in her life over fear and doubt. Sharing from her private struggles and victories, Elizabeth provides a roadmap for those who would like insight into their wilderness and trials. With lots of intentional questions sprinkled throughout, she has left behind roadmarks for the weary Christian to find the light to help them overcome the lies that might be holding them back. This book can illuminate their way to hope, deliverance, and freedom."

—Angelise Schrader
Author of *Live Out Love:*
Our Witness Speaks Louder Than Our Words

"In *Illuminated While Waiting*, Elizabeth Hughes offers a heartfelt and honest exploration of what it means to trust God's timing while waiting on His promises. Through personal stories and biblical wisdom, she guides readers to recognize God's light in their own waiting seasons, providing practical strategies for maintaining faith when circumstances feel uncertain. This book feels like sitting down with a trusted friend who understands your struggles and gently reminds you that you're not alone in your journey of faith."

—Taylor Phillips
Author of *Training Ground, From Anointing to Appointing*

Dedicated to...
My Worth Waiting For

Table of Contents

Introduction 11

One: Revelations Of Light & Waiting 19

Two: Seeing And Hearing God Speak While Waiting 43

Three: False Labels Turned Into Masterpieces 63

Four: Believing God & Looking Like A Fool 81

Five: The Good Shepherd 99

Six: Blessings in the Waiting 111

Seven: No One Can Disqualify God's Word 127

Eight: Shut the Door to Insecurities 141

Nine: Waiting Expectantly & Steadfastly 155

Ten: Waiting at the Well 169

Eleven: Illuminated & Lit Up 181

Notes 203

Acknowledgments 207

About the Author 211

Introduction

What is it about light that intrigues you? If you are anything like me, the light draws you in to see what is no longer hiding in the shadows. Have you ever contemplated why light pulls us in? Light illuminates everything surrounding us and draws us to look closer. The light extracts you out of the darkness. It pulls your attention to the promises of how vast God's love is by revealing how His promises never fail. The definition of light is; "the natural agent that stimulates sight and makes things visible: *the light of the sun.*"[1] I have always loved how light casts out darkness and removes the fears that try to linger. Light reveals the beauty of a new morning and provides joy when you are drawn into the sun's glow. The astonishing thing about light is that you cannot hide it. It removes the fear of the unknown onto which we try to cling. God's light pulls us from the darkness of what we once were, to walk in the light as His children. His light draws us in to become more like Him as chosen and set apart from this world. God's light heals us from our sinful pasts and gives us restoration to walk whole in Him alone. His marvelous light puts a fire in us to shine.

> *But you are a chosen race, a royal priesthood, a holy nation, a people for his own possession, that you may proclaim the excellencies of him who called you out of darkness into his marvelous light. Once you were not a*

people, but now you are God's people; once you had not received mercy, but now you have received mercy.
1 Peter 2:9-10 ESV

Strong's Exhaustive Concordance Of The Bible gives an excellent definition of the Greek word for marvelous light; *"Phos,"* which means "to shine, make manifest, luminousness, fire, and light."[2] God's light draws us in to shine and to be a fire for others to see. What a beautiful reflection of how powerful God's light and love is. The light puts us into a place of healing and restoration. His light heals the broken pieces of our lives and mend our hearts that need to be restored. When we are in God's light, we are healed from our past sins because He has wiped them away. Thus, being in God's light, we step into a stance of righteousness and leave the poverty mindset behind so we can walk out the healing God has given us. God heals us from the inside out to be made whole. His light draws us in to see Jesus as our healer and restorer. His light heals us to walk in love and to become imitators of Christ. As we are drawn into God's light and healed by it, we partner with God to bear the fruit of light. The things of disobedience and empty words are put behind us so we can discern how to walk in God's healing light.

Therefore be imitators of God, as beloved children. And walk in love, as Christ loved us and gave himself up for us, a fragrant offering and sacrifice to God. But sexual immorality and all impurity or covetousness must not even be named among you, as is proper among saints. Let there be no filthiness nor foolish talk nor crude joking, which are out of place, but instead let there be thanksgiving. For you may be sure of this, that everyone who is sexually immoral or impure, or who is covetous(that is, an idolater), has no inheritance in the kingdom of Christ and God. Let no one

deceive you with empty words, for because of these things the wrath of God comes upon the sons of disobedience. Therefore do not become partners with them; for at one time you were darkness, but now you are light in the Lord. Walk as children of light (for the fruit of light is found in all that is good and right and true), and try to discern what is pleasing to the Lord. Take no part in the unfruitful works of darkness, but instead expose them. For it is shameful even to speak of the things that they do in secret. But when anything is exposed by the light, it becomes visible, for anything that becomes visible is light. Therefore it says, "Awake, O sleeper, and arise from the dead, and Christ will shine on you."
Ephesians 5:1-14 ESV

There is no darkness in God. Since we are in Christ and have the Holy Spirit, the light of Jesus is in us. Once we know we are healed and restored by God's light, we can share the healing restoration of God's light. It is a shift of perspective of our identities in Christ. Knowing we are whole and restored by God's light, we become lights in the darkness, spreading the gospel's good news to those who need it. We cannot hide in the dark because we are a light (Matt 5:14). In the light, we are drawn back to God's majesty and away from ourselves. To become messengers of light and show how God's light removes the fears in our hearts.

This is the message we have heard from him and proclaim to you, that God is light, and in him is no darkness at all.
1 John 1:5 ESV

Each of us is unique because of who we are in Christ. Jesus Christ has given us His light through the Holy Spirit, who shines brightly within us. We cannot hide the light that God has put in us.

Throughout this book, I will share the revelations of light God gave me during my journey of waiting. Every chapter reveals the truth God has illuminated for me to see and believe. In the beginning, I will show how God gave revelations within my life and how you can see the same in your own. As you dig deeper into stories of my waiting, you will see how God's light frees us from fear and shows us how to release control to Him. The more you explore my voyage of waiting, the more you will know how to reframe your thoughts towards God. You will be able to walk with the mind of Christ God has given you. As my journey unfolds, you will be able to see God move while I wait. Sharing a portion of my waiting experiences, I will display how God broke my agreement with these false labels by flipping them into masterpieces, holding onto God's promises to take Him at His Word while looking foolish to the world. The middle of this book shows the importance of being led by the Shepherd to recognize God's voice, which keeps us steadfast while waiting. You will have the tools to learn how to persevere and to remain grounded in your faith. Continue reading; you will not want to miss out on seeing God's goodness. I will give a glimpse of how Job's story relates to my journey of waiting in many different ways.

Besides understanding the blessings of waiting, we will see how God's Word is not to be disqualified by anyone. On this pilgrimage together, we will learn how not to be easily persuaded in our faith and how nothing is wasted in waiting. These tools will show how we can shut down insecurities. Relating my story will help you see how to walk into any room with the authority God has given you. Later in the book, I will show how waiting expectantly and steadfastly brings hope. I share strategies with you to be able to walk out your waiting season with confidence. In sharing how God met me where I was, at the *"well"* waiting on His promises, you will get to see Jesus meet you where you are. When you are at the *"well"* with Jesus, you will find healing, restoration, and wholeness. You will begin to see how God speaks to you with intention. As we go further into this journey together, we will find these truths. In the last chapter, I will share how illuminated and lit up my life became after believing what God spoke to me. We will break down these disclosures to see the truth and be able to recognize the lies that try to get us to doubt the revelations of light. This journey is full of adventure, waiting with Jesus as He illuminates our steps...

As you come alongside this expedition to read my story, I pray it gives you hope to see and believe God with expectation. May it be a story of restoration allowing you to see God's light always leading you in truth and encouraging you to pick up your lantern and follow Him. Before we step into my journey any further, I want to invite anyone who has not accepted Jesus to have the opportunity to receive His light. All one needs to do is confess their sins to God, proclaim He is their Savior, and accept His gift of salvation and love. It comes down to the realization that we require a Savior. Pray this simple prayer with me: Jesus, I confess I am a sinner in need of a savior. I cannot do this on my own because I need your saving grace. Come into my heart and change me because I cannot save myself; only you can save me. Be my Lord and Savior, amen.

Digging deeper into my story, you will find waiting for promises to come is hard. It can feel like the anticipation of Christmas morning; we must learn to wait for dawn to come to open the presents of God's promises. Sometimes, waiting for the morning can seem long and drawn out. However, the wait is worth it every single time. See, every day is new. Each day comes with a choice to believe in God or give in to doubts. It comes with a sunrise and a sunset that looks different each time.

The beauty of each new day is filled with light and a unique opportunity to wait with anticipation for God's promises to come to pass. With expectation, we must remain in the light each day. As we dive deeper into finding illumination, we will learn how the light has multiple meanings within the journey of learning to wait.

> *You are the light of the world. A city set on a hill cannot be hidden. Nor do people light a lamp and put it under a basket, but on a stand, and it gives light to all in the house. In the same way, let your light shine before others, so that they may see your good works and give glory to your Father who is in heaven.*
> Matthew 5:14-16 ESV

Chapter One

Revelations of Light & Waiting

We have all had irrational fears many times as children. As a child, I was terrified of the dark and what was lingering in the unknown. I could not see past my bed, and there was no light to illuminate my room when the lights were off. The pitch blackness of the night was overwhelming at times, and I was afraid there were monsters under my bed. Despite having my parents check for these "monsters," I did not have peace of mind. Laying in bed in the dark, waiting to fall asleep seemed like it took forever. The unknown in the dark is what made me afraid. This fear of the dark was a stronghold on me I did not realize I had. The vastness of the dark kept me in this petrified fear of not knowing what was there because I could not see everything around me. As morning light came, it cast away the shadows to display there was nothing to fear. Just as I had to trust my parents when they told me there was nothing to fear in the dark, we have to trust what God speaks to us. The question is: how do we let God heal us of these fears to walk in freedom? It is important we learn to trust God with our fears and know He has already won the victory over them. It took me a while to let go of my fear of the dark and trust God. The more I realized God was trustworthy enough to take this fear away, the more I let go of being afraid in the dark. His love began to heal me of this fear by making it known to me there was nothing to fear. God's love poured into my heart and displayed how He was with me. The dark was no longer scary or daunting, It was just dark so I could sleep. Being in the dark was no longer about what I could not see but what I could see. Releasing this fear of the dark became about releasing my fears to God. Even though I had let go of this childhood fear, I still had a fear of the unknown.

Trusting God with my unknowns has been a battle. Letting go of my grip on everything so tightly and allowing God room to move was difficult. The more I began to trust God and let go of this fear the more I realized God is trustworthy with my fears and unknowns. Facing my unknowns has been about letting go of wanting to know when the rest of my life will start. When I would be married, how many kids would I have? This journey taught me to believe what God speaks over me despite my circumstances not changing instantly. Learning to trust God in the waiting was the first thing I had to do, and it was right in front of me. I had to work on waiting before I could go on to what was to come next. My waiting involved surrendering my unknowns to Jesus and trusting Him with an outcome I could not see. Holding fast to the light–the Word of God brought light to my unknowns because Jesus used the truth to shine His light on the fears I needed to release.

Choosing to relinquish my fears of the unknowns to God took conviction in knowing He was fighting for me when I was not aware of it. This is difficult when you have a fragmented heart full of fear. I spent a long time living with a fear of never being good enough. I didn't feel worthy enough to be loved and had to try to heal from having my heart crushed by the man I loved. While waiting with a heart full of fear, God showed me how to keep my faith by preparing me for what was to come. He was asking me to continually show unconditional love to the person who wounded my heart with fear. The man who is worth the wait. During this time, God helped me to hold onto His Word. He spoke to me to wait for the heart's desire of marriage and children to be fulfilled by Him alone. As I continued to pray for this man and laid down my unknowns–fears at God's throne, He showed me restoration is coming to pass in the shattered relationship and my fractured heart. I had to realize restoration may not look like what I think it will and lay it at Jesus' feet. Each prayer I prayed was an act of faith to let go of my own fear. As God was showing me to display unconditional love to this person, I had to trust God would not forsake me as I waited. I now know His Word proves true.

> *...fear not, for I am with you; be not dismayed, for I am your God; I will strengthen you, I will help you, I will uphold you with my righteous right hand.*
> Isaiah, 41:10 ESV

Waiting is a time of preparation where God readies us for what is next. It is not always easy waiting for God to bring us to the next step, but waiting for His best is worth it. Waiting is a time of refinement, where God opens our eyes to see what we are waiting for is worth the time and effort. By allowing God's Word to awaken your heart and letting Him light up your next step, you will discover things you never knew before. It is letting God's Word and light remove your fears and choosing to walk by faith. It is where God shows us the difference between the light in us and the light He uses to light the path before us. God purifies your heart in the waiting, stripping away what is not needed. The only thing that remains is what God has refined through holy fire.

Going back in time four years ago, I stepped out in faith into the light where God wanted me to travel to this conference despite the cost. The ministry hosting this conference was offering scholarships to those who could not afford a ticket; their website crashed many times as they were flooded with scholarship applications. Getting a scholarship was going to be no short of a miracle, but after several nudges from my amazing mother, I put in for a scholarship. God prepared my heart to attend "Lit," a women's conference in Houston, Texas, for women ages twenty through forty who are writers, bloggers, and speakers. Now, being in the mitten state we call Michigan, I never thought it would be possible to go to this conference in Houston. I knew the airfare would be pricey, and I had no idea what it would cost me to eat and have coffee while on the trip. I was deeply afraid of not being able to go to this conference. But I knew deep in my Spirit God wanted me there.

In addition, I thought it would be impossible to travel by myself for the first time. Truthfully, I was petrified of getting on a plane. Let me tell you, traveling is completely different when you are by yourself. I was nervous about flying and worried I would miss the plane or lose my luggage. I realize losing my luggage would make a great Hallmark movie, but thankfully, God had other plans than a ridiculous movie plot.

By God's provision, a wonderful friend blessed me with money for the airfare. God provided me with a scholarship through Lifeway to attend the conference. God supplied what I needed to attend the conference, which is a testament that God can do the impossible even now and flip circumstances for our good to remove our fears. So, if you need a reminder that God's provision is not late, here it is. Despite tiny setbacks during my trip to the conference, God continued to astound me with how His favor was everything I needed. God supplied a wonderful friend to room and share the adventure with, along with making many new friends. It was an incredible event and one I will never forget. It pushed me to grow spiritually outside my comfort zone, to move past the fear in my heart, and experience God's freedom. And, just for the record, I did not miss the plane or lose my luggage!

During one of the worship sessions at the conference, I had a defining moment when God whispered something over my heart: "I will illuminate what is before you, what is behind you, and what I have already put in you."

This word from God brought me to tears and overwhelmed my spirit. I could not contain the joy and release of peace that came over me after I started soaking in His words. That was just one of the treasures that God spoke over me through the Holy Spirit at this conference. (I will get to some other treasures later on.) I did not realize immediately that God was asking me to step out into a different position of my calling. I was a youth ministry volunteer; that is what I knew, but He was awakening the fire within me to write and speak to others about His love through blogging, writing, and speaking engagements. I am the kind of woman who has always seen herself as one who is good at being behind the scenes. The reality is I was hindered from stepping out in faith. Fear had blinded me, and I could not see where God had equipped me for this.

Jesus called me to step out and glorify Him, revealing to me what He had already put within me. God wanted me to make room for what He was doing, but I did not understand what He was trying to unveil. God was calling me to share my journey of waiting with those in similar struggles.

Meanwhile, I was mentally stuck in a mindset that I was "just a youth ministry volunteer" through working as a youth leader for freshman girls in a church ministry during my time in Bible college. I felt stubbornly stuck in a volunteer role perspective instead of openly following God's lead in other ministry outlets through writing. God had different plans for me, and I was too stubbornly afraid to step out in faith. I had to allow God to change my heart and mind about what ministry could look like through His eyes, not my limited, finite perspective.

Stepping Out in Faith–Letting Go Of Fear

I found peace in God's light by stepping out in faith and releasing my fears to God. His peace began to pour out over me when I was obedient to Him in sharing my faith. Two months after the "Lit" conference, I chose to be brave. I started a blog to share my journey of faith. I wanted other women who struggled with their identity in Christ, those who experienced fear, insecurity, or anxiety, to know God was with them. It was not easy because it required being vulnerable and sticking my neck out there, opening myself up to judgment and rejection by others. Having been hurt and rejected so many times before, I told God I was not sure I could do it again.

But in prayer and waiting expectantly for God, I had to put aside all my fears to hear Him. I positioned myself daily in a place to wait on God by sitting in His presence and opening my heart to Him. I had to be humble enough to wait upon the Lord instead of allowing frustration and pride to run rampant in my heart and mind. Within two months after the conference, God gave me the courage and peace to write a blog about my faith journey in Christ. The funny part is that the end of the two months happened to fall on the day before my birthday, April Fool's Day. So, go figure; God does have a sense of humor. God wasn't playing an April Fool's joke on me but showing me it's okay to laugh along our faith journey. The importance of this lesson of stepping out in faith is realizing God prepares you for the move. The humor in it is knowing that sometimes silly days or things can bring glory to God, too.

Stepping out in faith is never easy because it pushes us outside our comfort zones. We bear the fruit of the Spirit by aligning with God's word. During those two months, I had many fears and doubts about starting a blog to share my faith. I feared what people would think of me. If they would laugh at me, and even if they would reject me for being so open and vulnerable with my faith.

I do not turn aside from your rules, for you have taught me. How sweet are your words to my taste, sweeter than honey to my mouth! Through your precepts I get understanding; therefore I hate every false way.
Psalm 119:102-104, ESV

This step of faith was an action of letting go of my fears to step into sharing my faith. Yet, I did not realize God had already put in me what He wanted me to give, which was the brave confidence to write the truth of my waiting journey. He showed me I already had the words to write. I needed to pen down the words the Lord put in my heart to share. Fear hindered me from remaining steadfast to follow God's words and His calling on my life. I did not recognize this sooner because I was stuck in waiting mode, but He was saying, "The time is now." God had to reposition me physically and align my heart to hear the sweet words He was speaking over me. If we are not positioned to hear God, we need to check to see if our hearts are turned away from God or toward Him. It is about having a posture of humility before God, allowing us to remain steadfast before God. Humility helps us to see our fears are no longer a stumbling block. It requires laying down our pride–realigning our hearts by letting God lead us. Choosing humility is realizing you need God more than fulfilling the desires of the flesh, and your need for God outweighs your fears.. In this viewpoint, we can stand against the lies of the enemy because we have been rooted in humility before God. Positioning ourselves to hear God requires us to remain steadfast in our faith to let go of our fears. A stance of humility while waiting allows the lies of the enemy to be exposed, so we know the truth of how worthless fears no longer hold us captive. In faith, we can release our fears into God's hands and grasp the truth. We choose humility by asking God to humble us. A choice of humility also involves releasing our fears to God. Fear puts us in focus instead of God being the focus. We must ask Him to reveal where we are not being humble in our lives and to remain steadfast and not distracted by lies. It is realizing pride has no room in our lives when we choose humility. Once we choose humility, we can remain steadfast because it is tied to our obedience in humbling ourselves before God. This is where I asked God to give me strategies to choose a posture of humility.

Strategies:
1. Ask God to reveal where you are not choosing humility.
2. Write out what fears and lies you've believed so they no longer distract you.
3. Pray for God to help you release fears and choose a posture of humility more quickly.

I have been studying to posture myself in humility to hear God's sweet words these past few years. Before, I was waiting while God was preparing and positioning to appoint me. But first, God had to refine me for what was coming next. As I was being refined, God was showing me how the posture of humility was increasing my faith to hear His voice more clearly as I waited. Being in this place of humility allowed me to see how beneficial it is compared to the times I jumped ahead of His timing. Now, let me be honest with you. I have jumped ahead of God in the past, choosing a cheap substitute instead of His will. This is when fear was telling me I knew better than God. I grew burned out and tired during those times. While God was refining me to hear the truth of His words, others were attempting to tell me the opposite of God's calling on my life. Eventually, I learned, as God purified my heart, how sweet His words were to me. His words became sweeter than honey. I began to hang onto everything He was highlighting in my life and learned from a stance of humility how much easier it is to receive what God was teaching me. No one else could tell me what God's calling on my life was.

A wise mentor in youth ministry once told me, *"No man or human being can tell you what God has anointed, appointed, and called you to do. That is under God's authority alone."* That was the best advice I had ever received in life and something I will treasure forever. It confirms only God has the power to anoint us and appoint us to the calling He has placed upon our lives. When I have heeded God's leading, it has been a sweet little whisper of His complete peace washing over my heart and spirit. God's peace cannot be contained or boxed up. It is to be enjoyed and something we find rest in. I truly appreciate this great advice because I know it comes from a place of humility. My mentor from college, who has learned to heed God's voice above all others, has shown me a posture of humility where we see God's calling on our lives clearly. This mentor taught me an attitude of humility keeps you in a place to hear God's voice where fears flee. I will keep this in my heart forever.

Praying In The Secret Place

There is something so sweet in having God whisper to you in a moment when you are filled with peace. God's peace surrounds us to release our fears to Him. Starting my blog was just one of those sweet moments and whispers of peace. Another moment was during the "Lit" conference, where Christy Nockels spoke during the prayer hour. She shared that how we go before God in our prayer closets and what we pray in secret will manifest before us in our lives outside of these sacred places. God sees and hears what we pray in secret. Even with our fears we try to hide, He will bless us as we abide and seek Him out in prayer.

> *But when you pray, go into your room and shut the door and pray to your Father who is in secret. And your Father who sees in secret will reward you.*
> Matthew 6:6, ESV

The secret prayer you have with God will manifest itself on a platform, whatever it may be. A platform does not mean just a pulpit; it can be anywhere God places you. There have been several things God has spoken over me in secret that have not yet manifested, but I believe and am ever anticipating them to come. In addition, the things God has spoken over me have brought many tests of doubt and disbelief that they are God's words. I've even had doubts about whether God could speak to me or, instead, whether they are lies spoken and twisted by the enemy. However, deep within my soul and spirit, I knew these things could not be spoken by anyone but God alone. Praying in the secret place is a revelation of God's light, where He will guide us and teach us how to pray. As we pray in the secret place, we are placing our faith into action by setting our burdens at the feet of Jesus in prayer. The more we pray to God and are in constant communication with Him, the more our prayers will align with His will.

Thus, we cannot thrive unless we are in a relationship with God and communicating with Him. If we do not pour our hearts before Him in the secret place, everything will remain bottled up. Living with pent-up emotions and unexpressed prayers is no way to live. I have tried living this way, where the lies and fears were eating away at me and failed miserably. But God saved me from myself through prayer in my secret place. God created us to be in fellowship with Him; He wants to make us whole again through our relationship with Him. The Father made us for relationships and community, not isolation. He created us to live in the light and not darkness and to uplift each other in the light of Jesus, not our jaded perspectives or perceptions.

Moreover, the light of God's truth will always uncover the sin hiding in the darkness. The light of God exposes sinful parts of our hearts needing refinement by God's fire. Sometimes, we try to hide behind fear because we are simply afraid of having our hearts refined. After all, He draws out the sin that is holding us captive.

The enemy will do everything within his limited power to distract us from being able to hear God more clearly. Satan wants to cripple us with fear and distractions to prevent us from thriving in the authority God has given us. He wants to destroy us, but Christ has given us the authority to make him flee and shut his mouth. Prayer helps us when distractions come. We can ask God to give us the wisdom to combat these attacks.

> *But he gives more grace. Therefore it says, "God opposes the proud but gives grace to the humble." Submit yourselves therefore to God. Resist the devil,*

> *and he will flee from you. Draw near to God, and he will draw near to you. Cleanse your hands, you sinners, and purify your hearts, you double-minded.*
> James 4:6-8, ESV

Journaling our prayers helps us keep what we need to be focused on in black and white. Once we start writing out prayers we can write out the fears we are holding onto. Having a logbook of prayers to God helps us to be more honest, not just with God but with ourselves. When we are completely honest with God and ourselves, nothing is hidden within our hearts. Baring our hearts before God helps us remain steadfast in waiting because we are less likely to lose hope in what He has spoken over us. If we cannot journal our honesty with God and ourselves, with whom can we be honest? God knows our thoughts even before we speak them. Waiting helps us to pray the deepest things within our hearts, while humility is doing work to purify our hearts from being full of pride as we wait for God to fulfill the promise that is to come.

Divine Interruptions—Giving Up Fear

Have you ever overscheduled yourself? I admit to being in this category many times. There was a time God interrupted me by telling me to rest and to be still in His presence. I was busy working from home and taking care of others, and I completely forgot to give myself rest. I dropped everything and drove down to the beach. I finally began to enjoy the summer sun while sitting in the sand reading a book. It was on this sandy beach where God reminded me to rest, cherish His creation, and be still in His presence. By God interrupting my plans, my over scheduledness, I started to see it was for my good. But I realized I had to let go of my schedule to grab onto the Lord's good plans for my life. If our timetable is focused on us and not God's agenda, we will miss some of the people God wants to bring into our lives. An interference from God is a way to help us give up the fears we want to hold onto. God interrupts us with His divine appointments so we can experience His love through the people He brings into our lives. By slowing down, we can have fellowship and relationships with other believers. During these interruptions, there are times when God shows us our fears are irrational. For instance, God would use someone to tell me how He is faithful. I have heard other people call divine appointments "divine interruptions." Sometimes, God uses those moments to surprise us and show us unexpected blessings through connections with others. In these interruptions, God surprises us in more ways than we could ever imagine. In my own life, God used different friends to encourage me throughout my waiting season to keep holding on to the promises God spoke over me instead of giving up. He continued to surprise me with how He can use anyone to do His will and work in ways we do not expect. God revealed to me these interruptions were a time to grab ahold of His promises and give up my fears. Many of these times when God surprised me, He was assigning people to give me words of confirmation to express the promises that were coming; they just had not manifested yet. Some of the surprises were friends sharing their experiences of seeing how God amazed them by speaking to them and fulfilling promises. God used divine interruptions to get my friend's attention and see the astonishing blessings He was bringing into their lives through His love in unexpected ways. This gave me hope to keep holding onto God's promises in this waiting season. These stories helped me see how God worked in unpredicted ways to build bridges of connection with others and strengthen my relationship with Him.

God is in the business of connecting and bringing people

together. God loves surprising us in unexpected ways. God builds connections through relationships.

Sometimes, God uses the people who sharpen us the most to get us to take the next step into our callings. They are there to help us loosen our grip on fears and embrace God's promises. However, if we keep those people at arm's length, we may miss out on a great opportunity for our faith to grow. Usually, we push people away as a defense mechanism to protect ourselves from pain. Other times, we isolate ourselves because fear is controlling us. But God does remarkable things with ordinary people. Letting people in and being vulnerable with those whom God is bringing into our lives allows us to experience amazing fellowship and personal growth. Sometimes, God is asking us to open up in fellowship with others to let go of our fears.

Releasing Control into Jesus' Hands

Our journeys of waiting are a time of releasing circumstances out of our control into God's hands, especially when we entrust people we love to Him. Still, we know God's plan is far better than ours. Liberating our control to let God have it is choosing to realign our expectations with God's truth. I cannot always fully grasp how much God knows simply because He is our creator. It is a mystery how great God is in how He does not give us the full details of the outcomes of our lives.

If we knew the whole script, we might choose the easy stuff and skip the hard parts to remain in our boring routines instead of stepping out in faith. We have to relinquish control and pick up our crosses daily to follow Jesus' lead. For instance, if I had known years earlier how hard it would be to wait for God's best while watching other people get married and have kids, I might have settled for less than because I wanted it so badly. But God has laid it on my heart to stand firm in what He spoke over me by following His lead in not settling or compromising. I stood firm in the truth to yield control and follow His leading, not mine.

And whoever does not take his cross and follow me is not worthy of me. Whoever finds his life will lose it, and whoever loses his life for my sake will find it.
Matthew 10:38-39, ESV

There is joy in relinquishing control over to Jesus. We gain revelations of the promises to come in waiting as God uncovers things to us along our faith journey. God reveals the next steps we need to take by lighting the way before us. We just have to have the courage to take the next step with Him. We have to have faith not to give up, especially when we face hard questions like:

Did I hear God correctly? Am I foolish for waiting? Is this refining season over yet? Is my heart in hiding? Am I wasting my time waiting?

The hardest question I keep facing is: *Is it my time yet?* It seems like everyone else is getting my heart's desire to get married and have a family. I do not share this to get you to sympathize with me or take pity. Instead, I share it because waiting with anticipation is extremely important in not losing hope.

Waiting can be hard and lonely. We have all had moments when we asked God or even pleaded with Him for things to change. I have had many conversations with God about whether it was my time and why He was taking so long. I had a plan for my life; I would be married by twenty-five and have kids by thirty. Since I was already six years past my time frame and plan, I was blunt with God and told Him He was a little late. Let me tell you, God has made it clear this is in His timing, not mine. I have learned what God promised me is worth the wait in the end. When I tried to control everything, thinking I knew best by choosing to compromise for less, it was a cheap substitute for what He had waiting for me. God continued to confirm to me that what He had promised was worth the wait. I can finally rest because God is faithful to His promises.

Relinquishing Control-Looking Back

Realizing we do not have complete control over our lives is quite humbling. The unraveling of God's promises within my story began in November 2016 on a wintry Sunday morning at church. Once service was over, I talked with my mom and a friend about how I was looking for a job. While I was in this deep conversation with both of them, I very clearly heard God speak to me through the Holy Spirit, awakening me to the man I am going to marry and how He is going to fulfill my heart's desire to become the wife and mother I've always dreamed of being. God did not give a clear date or time of where and when, but He revealed the relationship and person. I am waiting for this man who is worth the wait. Even though God revealed this man to me, I also had to learn this man has his own free will and does not have to choose me in return. I had to release control over this situation to God to allow Him to work things out for my good. God was teaching me if this man chooses not to be the man worth waiting for me, He will bring someone else to me to fulfill this role. When God first spoke this over me, I laughed at Him, thinking this was impossible and completely crazy. However, I came to find out the joke was on me.

When God revealed I needed to wait for this man, my heart began to open to giving love and being loved. I let my guard down to allow my heart and thoughts to change about this man whom God showed me. God shifted my heart from seeing him as a friend to seeing him as more. To see this man as worth the wait, the one who is worthy of being loved. As my heart was changing, I felt it was time to reveal my love and feelings to him. My heart broke because he told me at that time he didn't feel the same way. I regret when sharing my feelings for him, I could not express I loved him. The honest truth is I ugly cried. Yet, this man showed me grace in our conversation together. My heart broke, but God comforted me by showing me there was still hope because He kept confirming this man was for me. God continued to awaken me to how He set this man aside for me and to trust Him with the circumstances, displaying to me how He could do the impossible. He was persistent in showing me He would not leave me abandoned but bring me a man worth the wait, even if it turned out to be someone other than who He revealed to me in the beginning.

To say my heart was fractured is an understatement. I lost all hope. I was sad and frustrated with God about the situation during this waiting time. The urge to take things into my own hands was definitely on my mind. I could hardly eat or sleep with this ache of my broken heart, and each day reminded me how I ruined and messed things up in this relationship. And then the enemy kept throwing this thought into my head that it depended on me to fix things and restore everything. But God showed me how to put my hope in Him, not the lies, doubt, or unbelief. God showed me He restores the broken things, not me, by restoring my broken heart to wholeness one piece at a time. The funny thing is God continues to quiet my heart because this promise is coming to pass, and hearts will be changed. He reveals that hope is not lost because He never loses a battle. In demonstrating how restoration was coming, God also taught me to release more control to Him. The more I rested in Jesus, the more I could relinquish control into His hands and be okay with the outcome. I realize some will read this and think I am crazy, and some will probably relate better than others. But I am OK with it because I know since I am in Christ, I am not crazy but insanely in love with Jesus enough to trust Him with my heart's desire. During this time, I did have to learn to trust God and allow Him to reposition my heart, too.

Reflections of Releasing Control

Releasing control to God was a long road to walk. I did not want to give God room to take back control. There was a lack of trust within me, wanting to keep control of everything. Giving back control over my heart, back to God was a huge leap of faith I wasn't sure I was ready to give. My heart had been shattered into tiny pieces. It was a time of messy, raw emotions that were not pretty. My emotions were on a rollercoaster, from crying fits of sadness to extreme numbness where I thought I couldn't go on. The thought of fixing everything myself ran through my mind constantly, trying to come up with ideas of what to say. I wanted to restore what I broke and take control. I was a complete mess full of insecurities constantly flooding my mind. My mind was filled with thoughts of not being enough, of not being worthy of being loved.

Have you ever been gripped by fear before? It can paralyze you if you let it. My fear of never being the woman worth being pursued haunted me so much that the illusion of isolation appeared to give me comfort at the time. But it was not. I have never been one to boldly share my feelings or open my heart to just any man. The very thought scared me to death. I feared never being worth it because the man I was still waiting for was flooding my mind, and these thoughts tried to get me to doubt God's goodness. The spirit of rejection was heavy upon me. During this time, I realized that even in my brokenness, God was there, mending the pieces of my heart little by little, allowing me to see He was in my midst, continuing to work. Even though my heart was broken and a muddled mess, God comforted me to see I would not stay broken. God was showing me I am worth waiting for because He sent His Son to die for my sins to save me. God opened my eyes and illuminated my heart to see I am worthy of His love and show me He is in control. He wanted me to know releasing control to Him would bring me freedom. I just needed to reach out and grab it.

Giving God My Yes

Giving God your yes can be a challenge of letting go of control. Has God ever asked you to do a hard thing and give Him a yes? If I am honest, I did not want to give God my yes to release control to Him. God surprised me by asking me to not only pray for this man, reminding me he is worth the wait, but also asking me to give Him a yes to continuing to show unconditional love to this man, knowing he may not return it. This meant writing out prayers to wave a white flag with words of kindness in a note or a text as God prompted me to do it. When God asked me to do this, I was determined not to do it at first. But God kept asking me to say yes. Releasing control in this area and giving God my yes involved saying, "I am not in control. You are, Lord." Eventually, I did, and it was after I said yes to God, peace washed over my heart and mind and started to mend the broken pieces of my heart. I found healing in writing down my prayers for this man because I knew God loved this man more than I could ever love him. Besides, it is tough to be angry with someone you are praying would draw closer to God. After I started praying for this man, my heart grew to love him in a deeper way than before. I was seeing him in a new light. I saw woundedness behind the fear of being loved tied to the fear of not allowing anyone close enough to hurt me in return. I am guilty of those fears going down a rabbit trail in my mind. I've closed myself off from love because I have been afraid to let anyone near me. God and His gracious love have flooded those places in me. His unending love fills those gaps.

For example, God put the pieces of my heart back together by renewing my hope in His Word. He confirmed His promise is true in waiting for this godly man. The confirmations gave me the hope to hold onto what I did not see or understand, even when my circumstances did not change. They also gave me joy in knowing they were affirmations of God's unfulfilled promises in the beginning that waiting for the man worth waiting for is still worthy of my heart and love.

Even yeses that may appear insignificant to some are not insignificant to our God. Small things, even just a word from a friend, affirmed God was working in me and showing me each step. It is the word of our testimonies that strengthens our faith to keep saying yes. God was illuminating things within me, and the revelations of His light highlighted things I needed to see. Giving God my yes was putting my faith in action to release control to Him. My obedience showed by stepping out in faith and saying yes to God. My biggest hurdle was when God began to reveal my hidden fears and strongholds, which needed to be prayed over for a breakthrough to take place. For breakthroughs to come, we must be willing to say yes to God while He is revealing things in us. A revelation I have totally grasped is that if the man I am waiting for chooses to exercise his free will not to pursue me, God will bring someone else into my life who is worth waiting for. To be candid, I feel guilty for admitting this. I truly believe the man I am waiting for is the one I will marry. But I have to understand that we both have the free will to choose outside of where God is leading us. Each step of this journey, including being present in divine interruptions, releasing fears of rejection back into God's hands, and repositioning my heart to align with God, is an act of faith to believe in the revelations of God's light. These things prepared me to see how God speaks in the waiting. As I dig deeper into sharing my journey of waiting with you, I pray you can see how God is illuminating His light into your life.

Repositioned To Release Control

Amidst our waiting, God has to realign us so we can release control to Him instead of always thinking we know best. Sometimes, God needs to reposition our hearts to see that something we are doing or not doing might not be the reason we are waiting. Sometimes, the other people involved need to be awakened by God for the breakthrough to happen. Before then, we may have to wait while they learn from God, and He will illuminate what they need to see. Waiting for the other person to wake up can be painful. When their eyes are opened, it is like dawn arriving. A shift takes place. This is not limited to relationships but also new opportunities. Whether we are waiting for a new position or if God is asking us to pivot to do something else, we may have to wait for God to open the door for the new thing to come. In seasons of waiting, God brings revelations and confirmations to give us hope to keep going. When we get these revelations of releasing control, we need not throw them away but stand firm, even if we look foolish to other people. Trust me, it is just a matter of time before we look foolish to others when we are obedient to God. Confirmations are a reminder that God does not leave us but always remains at our sides. They are also a prompt of how faithful God is to His promises.

Confirmations are a reflection of the connections in how God brings people together. The part we play in following God's leading is saying "yes" to God and not running away or hiding from what He calls us to do. The other thing God asks us to do is to believe what He speaks over us. But we have to be okay with missing pieces and details. Missing details are not always bad. God does not give us all the details to protect us from things we do not need to know. It is also a time when God molds us into more of His image by stripping away our need to control things. When we don't know all the details, we can focus on what God puts before us first. Not having all the details gives us time to realize how God is trustworthy in the waiting season, and our hearts can rest knowing we're in good hands. The peace God pours into our hearts shows us He is trustworthy. It gives us the proof we need to believe God in the waiting. Confirmations are a testimony that God has not forgotten us but is repositioning us to see He is in control.

In the waiting seasons, we also learn how God reveals His light and shows us how to release things back into His loving hands. By doing this, we are humbling ourselves before Him by recognizing His ways as better than ours. For example, I was trying to physically position myself to be seen by this man, trying to create chemistry by buying pretty dresses to get his attention. I realized my folly, confessed my sin, and submitted myself to God's timing. When we realize this, we know God's plans are greater than anything we could ever do.

As human beings, we want to control the outcome to get what we want, no matter what we try to manipulate. Women also get a bad rap for trying to manipulate and control their circumstances. However, we do not have to live up to this; we can break free in Christ Jesus. We can rise in Christ to overcome and walk in the freedom of His unfailing love. He is our saving grace who lights the way. God is the one who takes what we release into His hands to heal our shattered hearts. He restores us spiritually and mentally in the waiting season so we can be whole again. God is the one who picks up the broken pieces of our lives and puts the puzzle back together. We are taking ourselves out of the mix by allowing God to have his way with us. In doing this, we are letting go of things outside our control. We are also letting go of trying to manipulate things and letting God be God. Just like I had to let go of trying to control everything for God to pivot me in a new direction.

Reflection Questions:

What is holding you back from saying "yes" to God?

How has God repositioned your heart?

Is God asking you to step out or reposition your heart?

Chapter Two

Seeing And Hearing God Speak While Waiting

There was a time when I did not understand I could see and hear God speak to me. As I shared in chapter one of how God spoke to me within my spirit of waiting for my Boaz, I realized God wanted to speak to me more. He wanted me to hear Him more clearly. God began to speak to me by displaying how all these past men in my life were Bozo's. None of them were the Boaz, who was worth the wait. The Lord made it visible how each man from my past was not worthy of my heart, how they did not deserve my love. The more God spoke to me, the more I was able to discern his voice clearly in reading His Word, hearing it come alive as I read and feeling God's presence through worship. As I drew closer to God, His still, small voice that gave me peace over my circumstances became crystal clear. God wanted to speak to me about the man who was going to be my Boaz. To show me He cared enough about me to fulfill my heart's desires. He wanted me to understand Jesus lit the way and guided me onto the correct path. Even though my waiting period was a time of preparation, He would not mislead me but would guide me into all truth while remaining close by my side. He refined me in the waiting to become more like Him. I learned to discern God's voice while waiting to see and hear Him speak. Seeing and hearing God speak to me in these ways made me fall in love with Him all the more.

> *Again Jesus spoke to them, saying, "I am the light of the world. Whoever follows me will not walk in darkness, but will have the light of life."*
> John 8:12, ESV

It is astounding how God speaks to us all throughout the Bible through His Son, Jesus Christ, and the Holy Spirit. How He speaks to us is so personal that His voice is undeniably true. When God speaks to us, He will speak in a way we'll understand. In learning to hear God's voice, we must use discernment to determine and test if it is God by asking the Holy Spirit to give us clarification on what we do not understand. When God spoke to me in an inaudible voice, I clearly knew no one else was speaking to me. Here in John 8:12, Jesus speaks to the disciples and the Pharisees about being the world's light. This applies to us today because He came down from heaven to save us from our sins and bring us the light. The light of Christ in us is different from the light God uses to reveal our paths. God reveals this light to us when He speaks to us in the secret place, which can be part of His promises. It can be supernatural discernment that sheds light on an area of our lives we have not seen before. What is revealed to us in our walks of faith is a spiritual epiphany awakening our hearts to come alive. Sometimes, half the battle is choosing to believe God speaks to you. In his book, *The Discerner, James W. Goll says, "We have been created in the image and likeness of God, and we are meant to grow in our spiritual hearing ability; we have been designed to listen for His voice and to comprehend what He is saying."*[3]

Have you ever had a moment when you knew that you had heard from God deep in your spirit? Were there doubts or lies that caused you to disbelieve God's spoken word? Was there fear holding you back? When God spoke to me about the man who will be my Boaz, the Lord revealed himself to me in a new way, showing me how He speaks to me as I am waiting. God opened my heart and ears to hear Him through the Holy Spirit. It was a mighty yet still, small voice. I was so blown away at first when I heard the Lord speak I laughed, thinking it was crazy, but my belief in Him speaking to me was half the battle. Whether it is a small whisper, a still small voice, or even an audible voice, God speaks to us. God speaks to us through people. God spoke this world into existence. God spoke and created us from the dust of the earth. God can speak to show us who is a Boaz or a Bozo. He can speak to you if you are willing to listen.

Afterward he appeared to the eleven themselves as they were reclining at table, and he rebuked them for their unbelief and hardness of heart, because they had not believed those who saw him after he had risen. And he said to them, "Go into all the world and proclaim the gospel to the whole creation. Whoever believes and is baptized will be saved, but whoever does not believe will be condemned. And these signs will accompany those who believe in my name they will cast out demons; they will speak in new tongues; they will pick up serpents with their hands; and if they drink any deadly poison, it will not hurt them; they will lay their hands on the sick, and they will recover. So then the Lord Jesus, after he had spoken to them, was taken up into heaven and sat down at the right hand of God. And they went out and preached everywhere, while the Lord worked with them and confirmed the message by accompanying signs."
Mark 16:14-20 ESV

To See And Hear God

God speaks to us all the time. We have to decide if we want Him to point out who all the Bozos are in our life so we can see the Boaz He is bringing is worthwhile. To do this, we have to determine if we want to make room for Him to move in our lives. The more room we give God to speak to us, the more we will hear what He is telling us is worth the wait. God's voice is displayed throughout the Bible, from Genesis to Revelation. Some people see what God is saying to them instead of hearing what He says. God has no limits to how He speaks to us. He will speak to us through His Word, through nature, through other people delivering a message to us. He even speaks to us through worship or in the quiet moments with Him.

As I shared in the previous chapter, I have had one of these sweet experiences of hearing God speak. It was such a defining moment of whether or not I would believe what God spoke over me. On that occasion, I could hear God so clearly. It was like His voice was audibly speaking inside my heart and mind. I knew it could not be anyone or anything else. Although God did not reveal all the details down to the minute or date, He did awaken my heart to see part of His plan. By choosing to remain grounded in truth and believing in the promise with anticipation, we gain faith full of grit to withstand the enemy's schemes. To this day, I am waiting for this spoken word and promise to be fulfilled. However, I did have to realize that even if it does not come to pass exactly the way I want it to, I still believe God spoke this specific word over me about this particular man who will be my Boaz.

Believing this promise requires determination to remain grounded in what God spoke. It also requires fervent prayer over the hearts of those who hear God's voice. It requires perseverance to remain where God has planted me and not waver in believing a lie from the enemy. God began to give me strategies to see and hear Him speak to me. Strategies to be equipped in seeing God speak in unexpected ways and hear Him clearly above everything else. I want to share these with you so you can draw closer to God. My hope is these strategies will help you recognize His voice quicker, that they will help you grasp what God wants to speak to you, and you will know He is always with you.

Strategies:
1. Sit in the quiet and listen for God to speak to you.
2. Go for a walk in nature or your neighborhood and ask God to reveal how He wants you to see and hear Him.
3. Put on a worship song or playlist and listen.
4. Quit talking and let God speak.

Having these strategies helped me let go of my preconceived notions of how I thought God could speak to me. These strategies opened the door for God's voice to be louder above all the noise of this world. Knowing these things helped me to trust what God was saying.

Waiting For Boaz, Not Bozo

Waiting for my Boaz and not a Bozo is knowing that God has me covered. I am waiting with anticipation for this word to come to pass, so much so I am bursting with excitement and renewed strength to press on. Even though it was back in 2016 that God spoke this specific promise to me, God is speaking revelations and promises yet to come. This includes those He showed me in 2017 at the women's "Lit" conference about starting my blog. I have not lost faith or belief in God's Word or His spoken promises. Keeping the faith is not always simple. My journey of waiting for God's promise to happen means not settling on less than God's best for my life, including not going out and dating some kind of Bozo instead of waiting for Boaz—Mr. "Perfect for me" has not been awakened yet to marry me.

Instead, it means remaining steadfast in faith and pure before God. I believe in the unfulfilled promise that is coming because I see what God said is true. This journey of waiting for God to fulfill this promise over my life makes me relate to Ruth in the Bible. She approached Boaz at the threshing floor to be her and her mother-in-law Naomi's kinsman redeemer and did not go after an ungodly man.

So she went down to the threshing floor and did just as her mother-in-law had commanded her. And when Boaz had eaten and drunk, and his heart was merry, he went to lie down at the end of the heap of grain. Then she came softly and uncovered his feet and lay down. At midnight the man was startled and turned over, and behold, a woman lay at his feet! He said, "Who are you?" And she answered, "I am Ruth, your servant. Spread your wings over your servant, for you are a redeemer." And he said, "May you be blessed by the LORD, my daughter. You have made this last kindness greater than the first in that you have not gone out after young men, whether poor or rich. And now, my daughter, do not fear. I will do for you all that you ask, for all my fellow townsmen know that you are a worthy woman. And now it is true that I am a redeemer. Yet there is a redeemer nearer than I. Remain tonight, and in the morning if he will redeem you good; let him do it. But if he is not willing to redeem you, then, as the LORD lives, I will

Seeing And Hearing God Speak While Waiting

redeem you. Lie down until the morning.
Ruth 3:6-13, ESV

In learning to see and hear God speak to me in this waiting season, I now understand what kind of man God is leading me to and which kind of man He is leading me away from to keep me safe. The ones He has led me away from would have been stumbling blocks of Bozos that would have left me tripping over their stupidity. I remember the day before my twenty-third birthday. I went out on a date with an older guy who was in his thirties and from Chicago. Honestly, agreeing to go on a date with someone the day before my birthday was not a good idea. The one thing I remember was how horrible and awkward it was. I met him at a restaurant when I was out having dinner with my parents before I ever agreed to go on a date with him. The age difference did not bother me. The red flag I should have seen and recognized was how brazen he came across to me in asking me out right in front of my parents. I met this guy for coffee and pie, but what I learned was he was only after one thing and was not interested in really respectfully pursuing me. Thankfully, God protected me and lifted me out of the situation by helping me recognize this guy's real intentions. I am thankful I discerned enough not to allow this guy to steal my first kiss from me. In all of this, I learned what kind of godly man with whom I want to share my life. But I also learned how to hear God speak to me through the Holy Spirit, telling me to run when this guy turned out to have wrong intentions. This experience taught me that Bozos are not worthy of my affections. The promise is worth waiting for and is better than settling for what is less than His best. God's best is always worth the wait.

Reframing Your Mind For God To Speak To You

After arriving at the conclusion of knowing who God was leading me to, I needed to reframe my mind to allow God to speak. In humbling myself to hear God clearly, I readjusted my focus to put Him first above my desires in this situation. As I am anticipating for God to move, I want to be clear that waiting for the promise to come is hard. I am standing on God's Word, which does not and will not come back void. It arrives at the appointed time with anointing, which means I have to change my thinking to put it back into God's hands so I can let Him speak over the situation with restoration. The best thing I can do is to pray about it and to let God speak to me. By telling God my frustrations in the situation, I am laying them down at His feet, to hear Him speak to me. In praying about it, I am realigning my attitude and heart to submit to God's will and not my flesh. I am taking what He spoke over me and what He started in the spirit and submitting to Him to hear the new things. The alternative would be to remain in the flesh and allow my thoughts to dwell in fear. Prayer allows my heart to be renewed and realigned with what God started in the spirit so I can see and hear God speak to me. Prayer aligns me to know the truth in how God speaks in the waiting.

However, I want to clarify this: when God speaks over us, we must be humble to obey Him. When God speaks to us, we need to restructure how we look at our situations. We must be quick to respond, like sheep who know their shepherd's voice. Otherwise, we may be filled with regret and guilt for not following sooner. Regret can look like chasing after a Bozo rather than waiting for our Boaz. We do not need all the details to follow God, we just have to trust that He has all the plans safe in His secure hands. To be completely honest, this is hard for me. There have been plenty of times when I asked God for a specific "neon light" sign of confirmation but only got a quiet reassurance to remain where I am in continuing to seek God in the secret place.

This is still true when doubt or unbelief try to flood my mind. Have you ever had conversations with God where you just want a neon sign of which direction or step to take next? Well, you are not the only one. We all have had times like these. Where we are still in the process of focusing on what God is speaking to us. But we do not always get those kinds of signs. Most of the time we get small signs and simple miracles to believe in God. The more we dig deeper into what waiting seasons look like, the more we will see miracles to believe the truth for ourselves. Most importantly, we must remember that God will speak, light the way, and show us the next step. God will not forsake us and is right there in the middle of the mess and grit of life, illuminating—reframing what we need to hear. The middle of our story is as important as the beginning and the end. It is in the middle where we begin to learn how to hear God speak to us and stand firm in the truth. This was a huge process for me to begin with. I sloughed off what God spoke over me by not taking it seriously enough. I regret not heeding and recognizing it swiftly. After God first spoke to me about the man who is worth the wait, I remember laughing at God, saying it was impossible, like the way Sarah laughed at God in the Old Testament (Genesis 18:10-14). But I am thankful that God's grace covers me when I miss the mark. Yet, in every step I have taken in my waiting journey, God has been guiding me with His light, which means I am never alone.

While waiting, we must make room in our hearts and minds for God to move and light up what we cannot see or understand yet. If God gets blocked out, we will end up stuck in the past and unable to hear God speak in the waiting. The middle of our journey is where God strips away the things we do not need spiritually and physically so we no longer hang onto those crutches.

Reframing your mind for God to speak in your life and heart means humbling yourself before Him. God needs space to soften the hardest of hearts to be able to hear Him speak. If our hearts are crowded with things, schedules, or just plain busyness, we will be distracted, not directed or led by God alone, but by the flesh. Waiting for God to fulfill His promises, we must change our perspectives to be aligned with God's truth through prayer to see and hear Him. Otherwise, we will be solely focused on what we do not have or even what others have while we are in the waiting period.

Reframing And Journaling Prayers

Journaling the promises God has spoken over me is a tool I've used to stand firm in the truth. It is a tool I have used to restructure how I see things, to reframe how God wants us to view faith and pray. While in the waiting, remaining firm on what God has spoken means trusting God in the day-to-day tasks. It involves remembering what God spoke and journaling our prayers so they are deep within our hearts where nothing can dissuade us from God's truth. This is something I have had to do many times to get my heart in a position to believe God so completely that nothing could distract me from the truth. Just like Abraham believed what God spoke over Him about becoming the father of many nations, it is about becoming fully convinced through faith. That is exactly what Abraham did in obedience to God. He picked up everything to follow God to a nation he did not know. The belief Abraham had in God astounded me. Abraham took God at His Word and believed God was telling the truth. He trusted God to provide everything for him, which included all of his needs and his family's needs. Abraham waited where God told him until God told him to move. Abraham's faith in God was counted to him as righteousness because he remained steadfast in his faith.

> *By Faith Abraham obeyed when he was called to go out to a place that he was to receive as an inheritance. And he went out, not knowing where he was going. By faith he went to live in the land of promise, as in a foreign land, living in tents with Isaac and Jacob, heirs with him of the same promise.*
> Hebrews 11:8-9 ESV

The framework of my thoughts and how I see myself can affect how I see the waiting season. Creating a safe place to journal my prayers to God helps me become more vulnerable with God as I wait. Since God knows all and sees all within my heart and mind, I know I cannot scare God away with my sin or faults. He is not afraid of your or my imperfections. Instead, He takes those imperfections and uses them for good. He sees what needs to be reframed and changes it to bring glory to His kingdom. We do not have to be afraid of our imperfections or faults since God has already wiped away that shame. The question I had to ask myself was, "Why am I remembering what God has already forgotten about?" By journaling this question I was finally able to see how God had forgotten what I kept remembering. Those insecurities were not what God wanted me to remember or focus on. I was feasting on a table of lies, not on God's truth. God was chasing after me to sit with Him at the table of truth.

I kept stumbling over these insecurities that God had already forgotten about. I was feeding the insecurities by focusing on how I was not good enough and why I thought I was not worthy enough to be loved. I was struggling to reframe my thought life when God was trying to set me free. The stronghold keeping me captive in fear was the lie of how I was less than what God made me, compared to how God set me free from these insecurities and raised me from death to life through Christ (Colossians 3). The abundance of God's grace blows me away at times. He takes my shame of insecurities away to reveal how His perfect love covers me by removing the lies I have believed.

If then you have been raised with Christ, seek the things that are above, where Christ is, seated at the right hand of God. Set your minds on things that are above, not on things that are on earth. For you have died, and your life is hidden with Christ in God. When Christ who is your life appears, then you also will appear with him in glory.
Colossians 3:1-4 ESV

Lies Are Disarmed To Reframe Your Mind

God can do the same for your heart. He can gently remove what you remember because He has already forgotten it. He takes what we need to restructure within our minds so His love can wash over the lies and only truth remains. God disarms our defenses by removing our fears so we can be transparent when we pray and seek His presence. This is His way of being a gentleman and not forcing us to love Him. God removes the framework put on us by peeling back what is false so we can see the truth by finding the root of the lies we believe and digging them out. He peels back the enemy's lies of "almost truth" and replaces them with truth so we no longer have to feast or sit at a table of lies.

For us to realize that lies hold no value, we have to remember God's Word still stands. His Word is what we need to be feasting on at the table of truth. His word is what we need to be resting in, not anything else. We have to come back to God, not the lies. We must remember we are raised with Christ from the dead. Our old sinful self is gone, and we are made new in Christ. In allowing God to disarm our defenses, we have to renew our minds on things that are above, not on earthly things. When we see the actual truth, we see how God speaks to us in the waiting.

Renewed-Reframed Minds To See God Speak

Renewing our minds means taking time to be in the presence of God. His presence reframes how we see God speak into our situations. Whether it is in worship, in nature, at church, sitting on our front porches watching rain fall, He speaks to us. As our minds are reframed, we are taking the focus off ourselves to put it on Jesus. This changes us for the better. We become more refreshed to see how God speaks in our waiting seasons and more on fire to wait with hope. I have realized that when I am in His presence, my spirit has more peace than when I am focusing on the things in this world. In meditating on the things that are above (Colossians 3:1-4), I can focus on seeing what or how He is speaking to me. There is a transformation that happens when sitting in His presence where we become so renewed, distractions fade away. This is where we can sit in stillness with God as He disarms the lies. We gain a renewed hope to rest in Jesus.

Sitting in God's presence is where we can draw near to allow God's Spirit to fill our hearts and where our minds are renewed with a fullness of peace. As we are revived, we become stronger in our faith, because His love has removed what is hindering us. This is why sitting in God's presence is so important. He fills us with the Holy Spirit, renewing our own spirit in the process. His truth and promises set our minds on things above, not things here on Earth.

It is in the presence of God I become marked by God so people can see the difference in me. In the throneroom of God is where He reveals what I need to see and hear. It is here in His presence where His light marks me to shine brighter for others to see. I have had many experiences meeting new people who notice I am different from other Christians they have met. Their lens of God's love is reframed in a new luminosity. These people have told me how wonderful it is to see someone speaking the truth in love. They see God's radiant light shining on me through the power of the Holy Spirit renewing my mind each day. As I wait and sit in God's presence, becoming marked by God's spoken Word over me, is when His light renews my mind to believe only truth.

> *Since we have the same spirit of faith according to what has been written, "I believed and so I spoke," we also believe, and so we also speak, knowing that he who raised the Lord Jesus will raise us also with Jesus and bring us with you into his presence. For it is all for your sake, so that as grace extends to more and more people it may increase thanksgiving, to the glory of God.*
> 2 Corinthians 4:13-15 ESV

Our lens of God's love is restructured to see our righteousness is in Jesus not ourselves. In the presence of God, we find freedom to speak freely while we are sitting at His feet. While we sit in the throneroom with God, we can rest in His love. The presence of God gives us refreshment to see His grace extend to everyone. This refreshment reframes how we see others so we can extend grace. There is another verse in Psalm 27 about His presence I want to share with you. I chose this verse when I was graduating high school. This verse has been very powerful and a strength to me in good times and hard times.

> *One thing have I asked of the LORD, that will*
> *I seek after; that I may dwell in the house of the*
> *LORD all the days of my life, to gaze upon the*
> *beauty of the LORD and to inquire in his temple.*
> Psalm 27:4 ESV

Seeking God and His presence gives me supernatural peace that allows me to withstand anything that comes against me.
Reframing Our Thoughts

The process of allowing God to reframe our minds takes a determination to surrender to Him. One of the hardest parts of the waiting season is how drawn out, or long it seems. I remember when I was a teenager and taking driver's ed. I was not nervous getting behind the wheel, but I was a little intimidated in the beginning. The process can seem long-drawn-out with having to have fifty hours of driving time, plus several hours of classroom learning before taking the driver test. Sitting down in the hard, cold classroom chair in the public high school to take the written test was foreign to me as a homeschooled student. I greatly dislike taking tests because I get extreme anxiety when taking them. Taking tests can appear long and drawn out, but in reality, they are not that bad. We need to reframe our perspective and thoughts to look at things from God's perspective rather than ours. While I was taking the written test, every other student in the class finished their exams before I did, which means the teacher of the class was solely waiting on me to finish to be able to go home. In the back of my mind, I wondered if he thought I was dragging things out. When I got to the last question, I was more than relieved to be done; I think the teacher was too. Thankfully, I passed the written test and was able to take the road test to start driving by myself. Even though these things seemed lengthy, they were not. The preparation and the teaching I received allowed me to be equipped to drive safely. This is the same in reframing our thoughts in order to be equipped with the truth. Whatever you are waiting for can leave you drained because you become so focused on what is not yet fulfilled. It is like waiting in a doctor's office to get called back for your appointment. As you are in the waiting room surrounded by white walls that are cold and drab, the agony of waiting to get called back seems to take forever when, in reality, it is only a short time. The endurance we gain equips our minds to reframe our thinking to the things of Christ.

Not only that, but we rejoice in our sufferings, knowing that suffering produces endurance, and endurance produces character, and character produces hope, and hope does not put us to shame, because God's love has been poured into our hearts through the Holy Spirit who has been given to us.
Romans 5:3-5 ESV

It is in endurance that we find the strength to meditate on scripture to reframe our minds on what God wants us to do. I had to exchange the lies for truth and stop coming into agreement with lies. For instance, I learned to stop dwelling on how the promise I was waiting for was not fulfilled and see it was coming at the right time. I rebuilt my thoughts to dwell on God's Word and what God says about the promises, not just my finite perspective. By reconstructing my thoughts while waiting, I saw God was preparing me to become steadfast in my belief in Him, not within my circumstances. It is possible for you to reframe your thoughts by taking those thoughts of negativity and lies before the throne of Jesus and laying them at His feet. Choose not to pick them back up. Find the root of the thought or lie that is a trigger that puts you in a tailspin and test it against scripture. I guarantee the lie or thought will not hold up but fail every time. This is how we reframe our thoughts by meditating on God's Word and continuing to go back to it. I am going to challenge you with some homework to do.

~Write down the things you believe about yourself. If anything is negative, lay that lie down at the feet of Jesus. Then, dig for the truth in Scripture.

> *...looking to Jesus, the founder and perfecter of our faith, who for the joy that was set before him endured the cross, despising the shame, and is seated at the right hand of the throne of God. Consider him who endured from sinners such hostility against himself, so that you may not grow weary of fainthearted.*
> Hebrews 12:2-3 ESV

By focusing our minds on the blessings of expectation God has given us, we gain a clearer understanding of His promises. As we abandon negative things to cling to positive things, we are able to see His favor in our lives with illumination. Thus, if you are struggling in your waiting, whether it is a job, a relationship, marriage, or motherhood, rebuild your focus on Jesus. Rebuild your mind to dwell on the favor God has given you with gratitude.

In the waiting season, when we focus on God's word, we gain wisdom to see what God is illuminating before us. Sometimes, we need to renew our minds to be able to discern where God is bringing restoration in our lives. This is where discernment comes in. We always need the guidance of the Holy Spirit to lead us in truth so we do not lose sight of what God is calling us towards. Discernment gives us a sudden clarity to stand on what God spoke while waiting for our unfulfilled promises. Having discernment helps us reframe our minds to understand we are right with God. It gives us understanding we are no longer sinners but are saved by His grace to live in freedom.

When we reframe our thoughts in being renewed through the work of the Holy Spirit in us, we can see how we are raised with Christ and positioned with Him as heirs (Colossians 3:1). We are no longer sinners; we are saved. As God transforms us, we become kingdom-minded instead of dwelling on worldly things. Focusing our minds on things above, we are able to see we are raised with Christ and seated with Him at the right hand of God. Once we know we are raised with Christ, we can see the authority God has given us to no longer see ourselves as sinners but as redeemed children of God. As this revelation of redemption Christ has given us deepens within our hearts, we can live in a place of freedom to remain kingdom-minded. It is knowing with conviction you are an heir with Christ and not just believing it on the surface level. In my relationship with God, I have gleaned there is nothing surface-level with God. He has challenged me to dive deep into my convictions and beliefs by not wavering from being made an heir with Him. God has taught me to remain steadfast in knowing I am raised with Him and not lose sight of this truth.

But God, being rich in mercy, because of the great love with which he loved us, even when we were dead in our trespasses, made us alive together with Christ—by grace you have been saved—and raised us up with him and seated us with in the heavenly places in Christ Jesus, so that in the coming ages

*he might show the immeasurable riches of his
grace in kindness toward us in Christ Jesus.*
Ephesians 2:4-7 ESV

Since we are raised with Christ and hidden in Him, the renewal of our minds comes supernaturally through the Holy Spirit, who is working in us daily, so we become more and more like Christ. Our minds begin to want to be set on the things above because we desire to know Christ more. God reframes our thoughts by changing our desires to yearn for Him. The more our minds are trained on things above, the less the flesh wins. The flesh in us is put to death by the work Christ did on the cross. He raised us from death and seated us in the heavenly places with Christ. This is the evidence of God's grace being shed on us because He loves us. It is also evidence of seeing how God reworks us from the inside out, taking what we used to desire and making it unappealing. The desire for God becomes more important than our wants. He becomes our only desire. Our relationship with God shifts our focus, and everything else falls by the wayside. We begin to see Jesus as all we need, nothing else. Our minds become transformed to dwell in the truth rather than in the flesh.

Reflection Questions:

Do you believe God can speak to you?

How are you reframing your thoughts to reflect the truth?

What lies has God disarmed in your mind?

What prayers are you journaling?

Chapter Three

False Labels Turned Into Masterpieces

Have you ever been falsely labeled with something?

False labels can surely trip us up; it's easy to fall into the trap of believing lies someone has told us or lies we have told ourselves. These labels are not based on truth. For God's love to be poured into us, these labels need to be removed from our minds. When we surrender to God and let Him lead us, we can receive His love because we are willing. Being led by God means submitting to the Holy Spirit's leadership. It also means only speaking the truth and holding our tongues when we want to lash out or get revenge. After an experience in college, God unveiled this revelation of light to me by showing me the false labels I believed were true had nothing to stand on. He was uncovering what needed to be removed from my mind so His love could pour into my heart. But let's dive into this some more.

You can probably remember false labels someone tried to put on you, whether in school or something silly at camp. This could be related to gossip someone was spreading about you. It could even be a nickname that does not depict the truth about you. The point is labels put people in categories that limit others' perspectives about them. These false labels need to be poured out so God's love can pour into us. He must strip them away from us so our God-given identities are the only thing that remains.

I have experienced many false labels, but one that sticks out was placed during my journey of finding a good college to attend. I tried applying to a few traditional, secular colleges, but it was not the right fit. I knew my heart and head needed to be taught from a biblical perspective, so I kept searching for the right Bible college. I was aware I needed truth to be poured into my mind, and I knew God was calling me to ministry. Finally, I found a small Bible college, where I met some amazing friends and professors who challenged me to know God more. During my time at this Bible college, there was a person who tried to put a false label on me as being a hussy, meaning that I was only there to seek out a husband instead of being there to be obedient to the call God placed on my life.

This was a false assumption because that was not my motive for being in Bible college. I was purposely there to learn more about God, to seek out the calling He had placed upon my life through being equipped in ministry by learning to help others find their faith in God. The false labels this person was trying to spread made me feel insignificant and totally devalued, not just as a woman but as a human being. I was completely mortified someone would say those things about me because I thought this person knew me better. It also made me feel like my words held no value. When I did transfer to another Bible college, the year I spent there challenged my faith to start believing what God said above what other people were saying or thinking about me. This experience helped me see the value of truth being poured into us rather than lies. At this Bible college, I met one of the greatest mentors I have ever had in my life, who challenged me to believe in God and seek out His will above all else. He has given me strategies to wage war against the false labels I faced; these were the remedy to seeing where His love needed to spill into my heart. I want to share them with you so you are also equipped to fight.

Strategies:
1. Ask God to reveal any false labels you've believed about yourself.
2. Go to scripture and find truth to break these false labels and speak them over yourself.
3. Pray with the rod of authority God has given you to break these strongholds of false labels off of you.
4. Speak the name of Jesus over the chains of false labels, and they will bow down to Jesus.
5. Seek God and His righteousness by letting His love pour into you.

These strategies are intended to help you see where God's love needs to fill the empty spaces inside of your heart. God will pour out the false beliefs which need to be left unsaid by wiping away our sins. He does this through the gift of salvation. This is the power of salvation through Jesus Christ. The guilt attached to our sin or memory is removed from us. The power of God's love wipes away the shame that has held us in bondage for too long, which places us in a position of being fully convinced of God's truth. His unconditional love has unlimited power and cannot be measured. The pouring out of God's love never runs dry, which is why we have the ability to pour into others.

For God's love to pour out of us, we need to recognize the false labels and strongholds that have been holding us back. Strongholds can be dangerous because they keep us from seeing the truth, which is why we need Jesus to free us. The bottom line is that false labels are an entangled web of lies. To disable these labels and lies of the enemy, we need to know we are a child of God, not the lie someone told us we were. Jesus is the one who releases us from the bondage of the false labels–strongholds we have experienced. Salvation through Christ Jesus removes sin in our lives by eliminating the strongholds that have been lingering behind us. Jesus died on the cross for us and took our sins, shame, and guilt to release us into freedom through sanctification. This is the Holy Spirit working in us to purify us into becoming more like Jesus every day. In the daily process, God turns false labels into masterpieces by exposing them and removing them from us so we can walk in the freedom of His love and truth. The unbelief is divulged in us for God's love to pour and fill us with what is right.

Afterward he appeared to the eleven of themselves as they were reclining at table, and he rebuked them for their unbelief and hardness of heart, because they had not believed those who saw him after he had risen. And he said to them, "Go into all the world and proclaim the gospel to the whole creation. Whoever believes and is baptized will be saved, but whoever does not believe will be condemned. And these signs will accompany those who believe: in my name they will cast out demons; they will speak in new tongues; they will pick up serpents with their hands; and if they drink any deadly poison, it will not hurt them; they will lay their hands on the sick, and they will recover. So then the Lord Jesus, after he had spoken to them, was taken up into heaven and sat down at the right hand of God. And they went out and preached everywhere, while the Lord worked with them and confirmed the message by accompanying signs."
Mark 16:14-20 ESV

When God speaks to us, He will give us confirmations with

accompanying signs, provide us with clarification to stand on to wait on Him, and equip us to proclaim the gospel once He has removed the bondage in our hearts that needs to be broken off.

God enables us to obey what He commands when we are fully convinced of the truth. Being fully convinced is where we are fully soaked in truth and love God has poured into our hearts. Therefore, we do not have to look for other things to direct us because God is already directing us and leading us in truth. This is where having the grit to stand firm and let nothing dissuade us from believing God comes in. It also goes back to knowing our identity is in Christ, not this world, which means we do not need the world to tell us something different from what God has already spoken. We have to remember we can rely on God to come through. Most importantly, we need to remember that God's word still stands. It has not wavered or lost its power and will flow at the appointed time.

We need to rest in the fact God is leading us. His word is a lamp unto our feet (Psalm 119:105) and will never mislead us. It is a cascading light that never goes dim. His love continues to stream through us to display our identities sealed in Jesus. See, the world and culture want every single one of us dazed and confused about our identity in Christ. Yet, the fingerprint of God on His creation cannot be changed, nor can anyone thwart what God speaks over us. I point this out because nothing can slow down the pouring out of what God has already spoken. God's Word and His plan still stand. He remains faithful even when we fall short or lose sight of how God works in and through us.

This brings my heart joy in how trustworthy God is and how faithful He is in what He speaks. What comes forth from God is always good. Can we bask a little in how God does not lose any battles? He remains and always will remain victorious. God continues to prove Himself faithful all throughout my life. He will do the same for you. What brings joy to my heart is how we cannot be separated from God's love. This is confirmed in God's word in Romans 8. The thing is, once we accept Christ as our Savior, we become His. God gives us a new label as we become His children. We are made new in Christ. Our position in Christ can never change once we accept Him as Savior. The world and culture will tell us differently, but the false labels of this world can no longer linger on us. We are made righteous in Jesus. His love flowed over us and made us right with God.

No, in all these things we are more than conquerors through him who loved us. For I am sure that neither death nor life, nor angels nor rulers, nor things present nor things to come, no powers, nor height nor depth, nor anything else in all creation, will be able to separate us from the love of God in Christ Jesus our Lord.
Romans 8:37-39 ESV

This is the almighty power of God's unconditional love that changes us from the inside out. God peels back the layers of what is false so the truth can be seen and heard. False labels of comparison distract our minds from seeing the truth while we are in a waiting season instead of being rooted and grounded in the truth of God. When He removes the false labels of comparison, we regain our hope to wait with anticipation. A shift of focus must come in by taking our eyes off the circumstances and letting God tear down the stronghold of insecurity so our minds can wait with anticipation. If we are just focused on the circumstances beyond our control, we will not give enough room for God to restore them, nor will we be able to wait with anticipation if we are focused on what is not changing. Allowing God to move within the circumstances gives us the ability to focus on what is to come.

God has had to clear the clutter out of my heart and mind regarding what I thought about and how I saw myself, and the circumstances around me. He has had to flush away the idols, the insecurities, and the labels that other people have tried to attach to me or that I've even attached to myself that were based on lies. God had to unfasten the lies of *"I am not good enough, I do not matter, I am not worthy enough, I am not worthy enough to be loved by someone, I do not deserve to be loved, or I am not attractive enough to be married to a good looking man."* He had to detach the lies and false labels of compromise or comparison so He could fill it with the truth that what He already put inside of me was enough.

Pouring Out to Be Poured In

As God removes the lies of the enemy and the false labels people have tried to attach to our God-given identities, He has a way of restoring who we are and how we see ourselves so we can walk in the truth of His love. When God washes off the clutter and the crowdedness of our minds, our hearts can see ourselves through His eyes instead of our finite points of view. We have to grasp that when God looks at us, He sees Jesus in us. His love has immersed us in truth to where we can pour out His love into others. Through the Holy Spirit, God redirects us to the straight path He has called us to. God illuminates what is before us to see the truth more clearly. He does this by pouring His love into us to change our hearts from focusing on negative things to focusing on the truth.

For many years, I allowed the fear of the opinion of man and the lies they believed about me to become my own perspective, which was wrong. I began to devalue my identity and believed for quite a while that no one would ever love me because I was unworthy, which is just plain foolishness. I let the lies of the enemy muddle my identity, and I began to forget who I was in Christ even though I was saved. God had to uproot those lies from my heart and pour His love with the truth back into me.

Once God began to uproot those lies and renewed my mind with the power of the Holy Spirit, I started to believe in Him again. In this renewal process, He showed me I had to put the truth into action and stand my ground in faith instead of letting the enemy take the ground I fought for. He also revealed how He removed the spirit of rejection from me by showing me how loved I am by Him. God opened my eyes to the fact that I needed to remain rooted in the truth, not people's opinions or fear of man. He restored my identity so the false labels put on me crumbled against the truth of God. Here is some truth for you: God does not mislead us. He removes the false labels to pour in His truth and love.

> *. . .that, according to the riches of his glory, he may grant you to be strengthened with power through his spirit in your inner being, so that Christ may dwell in your hearts through faith—that you, being rooted and grounded in love, may have strength to comprehend with all the saints what is the breadth and length and height and depth, and to know the love of Christ that surpasses knowledge, that you may be filled with all the fullness of God.*
> Ephesians 3:16-19 ESV

God points us back to restoring our identities and how we see ourselves so we can walk in truth in His love. It is like He uproots the weed of lies and replants our hearts with truth. This is where being rooted and grounded in God's love comes in, so we can be strengthened to believe rightly and be filled with the fullness of God. We want to be overflowing with the truth so it can dwell in us richly.

But you are a chosen race, a royal priesthood, a holy nation, a people for his own possession, that you may proclaim the excellencies of him who called you out of darkness into his marvelous light. Once you were not a people, but now you are God's people; once you had not received mercy, but now you have received mercy.
1 Peter 2:9-10 ESV

When the clutter of false labels is washed away, we can finally see our true identity is in Christ. We can finally see the false things are poured out so His love can seep into the deepest crevice of our hearts to renew us. When we lay the lies at the feet of Jesus, we can see with fresh perspective how God truly made us to be set apart, not torn apart. We are a chosen people whom God came to save. We can also step into waiting with anticipation in the hope God has given us through His promises of bringing us out of darkness and into the light.

Therefore, my beloved brothers, be steadfast, immovable, always abounding in the work of the Lord, knowing that in the Lord your labor is not in vain.
1 Corinthians 15:58 ESV

I learned that God's view and opinion of me was better than my sinful thoughts of thinking of myself as less than. More than that, I learned that when I think of myself as less than others, it is considered a form of pride, which I was not okay with. I did not want to devalue who God created me to be. Whereas, if we believe we are better than others, we are making ourselves an idol above God. Neither is a healthy outlook. I learned by faith that standing on God's promises means not moving from where He has placed me. It means remaining firm in His love by not doubting. Dwelling on doubts and fears can lead to believing a lie about yourself. Instead, sit in His presence and allow His love to mark your mind with truth, letting the lies fall away.

Once I realized God was calling me to stay rooted and grounded in His truth, I could flourish in my calling to write. Once I gave up believing the lies, I could pour out what God taught me to others. Here is what I want you to take away from my example: when we hold on to the cheap lies of the enemy instead of believing God's truth, we lose the ground we fought for, and we fall back in fear. When we are in fear, we become paralyzed to the point that we do not know what to do next. We end up losing sight of all the love God has poured into us.

Walking in freedom of God's truth roots and grounds us in love. If we do not step out of the lies of the enemy and step into the truths of God, we will miss out on the blessings of God. But to do this, we need the refining fire of God to burn away the lies of the enemy and get to the root of where the lies began. This is where God begins to uproot them and replant the good roots that will grow the fruit of the Spirit by pouring His love into us. Once the lie is exposed to the light of God's word, then God's love is poured out on us to heal the wound. He awakened me to see this wound of not seeing myself as enough by opening my ears to hear how He made me enough in His image. When I finally learned I was enough in Christ, the lie of not being enough lost its hold on me. God healed me of this and restored my identity.

In January 2020, God showed me this during a time of physical healing after I fell and broke my right ankle. I was arriving at Awana for a night of volunteering on a cold, wintry night. For those who are unsure of what Awana is, it is a non-profit ministry of discipleship for kids to learn the gospel through memorizing scripture, learning bible stories, and interactive games. Heading down a dark staircase, I missed the last two steps and fell forward to the ground, hitting hard. When I was getting up to leave for the night, the pain of the fall hit me. I ended up having to undergo surgery, where two screws were put into my ankle. During this time of physical healing, God had to refine and peel back the lie the enemy began feeding me that I would not run again. Pouring into me the truth of who I was and who He created me to be, God burned away the lie I was believing. He had to plant healthy seeds of truth into my mind for me to see the enemy was lying as He healed me physically to run again. I proved the enemy wrong by listening to the truth of the Lord. In 2021, 2022, and 2023, I participated in a Thanksgiving Day Run held by the local YMCA, and I finished each race by making it past the finish line.

We must be willing to submit to the authority of God and let Him remove the false labels put on us by the wrong people, the enemy, circumstances, or experiences. I realize I just used a word many people cringe to hear: submit, especially all of my fellow sisters in Christ who also struggle with submission. No judgment here, sisters. I am right there with you. But following hard after God and being rooted in His love means dying to self, taking up our crosses, and following Him. Following Christ means giving up our flesh and selfishness to pursue Him. Letting go of false labels put upon you is done by dwelling in God's presence. Within His presence is where we will find spiritual rest in submitting to God's authority. And if we want to boldly step into what God has called us, we have to willingly be refined by the fire of God in submitting to His will instead of the flesh.

Do all things without grumbling or disputing, that you may be blameless and innocent, children of God without blemish in the midst of a crooked and twisted generation, among whom you shine as lights in the world, holding fast to the word of life, so that in the day of Christ I may be proud that I did not run in vain or labor in vain.
Philippians 2:14-16 ESV

Here's what I have learned in combating lies and insecurities that have flooded my mind and tried to distract me from the truth: hold fast to the word of God. Read it; "I am a light created by God to shine in this world to point back to the truth," memorize it. Moreover, put away grumbling, selfish ambitions, and disputing with others and with God, so we can hear Him speak louder than the enemy who is trying to disrupt our focus.

Believing What God Speaks

Do you ever find it hard to believe what God speaks to you?

Believing what God speaks involves having a deep trust in Him. It is a confidence in God that cannot be shaken. I have to be careful with whom I share what God has spoken over me because the enemy can twist their words and intentions for his wicked schemes to get me to disbelieve God. I had to get to the point of being so fully convinced of God's spoken promises and my identity in Christ that nothing nor anyone could ever get me to disbelieve what God said. I learned this the hard way in sharing some of the promises God spoke to me and learned not everyone believes God can speak to us. Through the process of trying to share God's goodness with someone, I learned how He is gracious with us when we have crooked unbelief flowing in our hearts. He shines His light in the dark places. God has also called me out of this crooked and twisted generation to shine as a light and expose lies and hypocrisy underneath the surface. To do that, I have to know *"whose I am,"* and where my identity comes from. My identity comes from God alone, although I have to be aware God is going to expose my faults before I can go before others to speak the truth over them. I have to recognize my sins and confess them before God before I can do anything else.

God is not afraid to call us out on our sins; we don't have room to be hypocrites or judgmental Christians who think we are better than others. God keeps calling us back to Him in pursuit of purity and holiness. He is calling us out of sin and back to repentance to draw near to Him, calling us to a place of deep faith in the truth to abide in His word, not the false things of this world. He calls us out of the darkness to step into the light of following Him.

God is calling us to be alone with Him, to get back to what matters by being in an intimate relationship with Him. He wants us to hear the rich words He speaks over us and wants us to believe them by taking action when we are given the next move. I will admit, there are times we have to move when God speaks, even if we do not have all the details. And there are times we must ask ourselves: will we trust God and follow what He speaks over us even if we look like complete fools to everyone else?

Believing what God speaks over us will test our faith and grit. It will also test the ground we fought for against the enemy and whether we will remain rooted in the love of God. The epiphany I had was when I believed what God spoke over me, I believed He was actually telling me the truth and it is coming to pass. This was a choice I had to make to believe each day.

Choosing to believe God speaks is not only an action; it is also a journey to discover God is faithful every single time. Believing God is a process just like sanctification is a process; neither comes overnight. The process looks like realizing what God says is true and standing on it, not allowing things to dissuade us from it. It means experiencing the promises of God's word, knowing that He never fails or lies. You can take that one to the bank every time. Believing God speaks also means stepping out into the calling He has placed on your life by being willing to stand in the gap when no one else will. We may not all be called to leadership, but God calls us all to step into the unique calling He has placed on our lives to spread the gospel. It is about taking the risk of looking foolish for God when everyone else around you thinks otherwise. By believing what God says, you are choosing to stand with grit rather than giving up. It is about standing up and standing set apart for what you believe. In being willing to stand out, we are beginning to take the step of building momentum in our faith to take God at His Word. This means we have to be humble enough to walk with integrity when no one is watching no matter what season we are in. In the process of God peeling the false labels off of you and pouring His love into you, He is awakening your heart to be faced with a choice of either drawing closer to Him or running from Him.

"And God has appointed in the church first apostles, second prophets, third teachers, then miracles, then gifts of healing, helping, administrating, and various kinds of tongues. Are all apostles? Are all prophets? Are all teachers? Do all work miracles? Do all possess gifts of healing? Do all speak with

tongues? Do all interpret? But earnestly desire the higher gifts. And I will show you a still more excellent way."
1 Corinthians 12:28-30 ESV

Standing firm in His word builds a foundation within our faith that will not shake, bend, or sway our belief in God but remain unwavering in faith. Believing our Father speaks adds to the steadiness we build by taking Him at His truth. In standing firm on His promises, we build a stronger wall of faith around our hearts to remain steady in the foundation we've built over what the Lord spoke to us. When we have a strong wall of faith around our hearts, we can dig deeper with God and be renewed in Him with fresh fire to rightly handle the word of God. By using the truth correctly, we can avoid irrelevant things that do not matter.

Remaining in a position of teachability gives God's love a chance to pour into us and to change us from the inside out. When He calls us out of hiding, it is our willingness to act on what He is asking us to do that submits us to His authority. When we share what He places upon our hearts, we receive a holy fire from God to be bold in sharing our faith instead of remaining silent. Watching over what God places on our hearts means avoiding things that do not matter, like irreverent babble and contradictions of the truth that will sway or take our hearts' attention away from God. Guarding the good deposit of faith gives us the strength to keep hoping for what is coming instead of looking at what is behind us. Protecting and guarding the good things entrusted to us means holding fast to the truth and not wavering from it.

Do your best to present yourself to God as one approved, a worker who has no need to be ashamed, rightly handling the word of truth.

*But avoid irreverent babble, for it will lead
people into more and more ungodliness.*
2 Timothy 2:15-16 ESV

Open your heart to what God has entrusted you to believe. Let your ears be opened to hear His sweet whispers of love. God has bestowed upon you the responsibility to protect and guard what He has spoken to you to believe. Be open to what God is calling you to step into without fear and doubt. Be fearless to believe God's spoken word. Unlock your mind to believe in the beauty of God's promises so your heart can be open to new things.

Allow God's love to pour into your heart and give you fresh fire to burn a bright light for others to see and want for themselves. Take God at His word so your heart can be unlocked and not defensive. Be open to His love pouring into the dark places in your life that need to be filled. Stop allowing the world to fill you with temporary things. God is waiting for you to believe in Him again. As you allow your heart to believe in new things, you will find a great sense of trust in God's faithfulness you have never experienced before.

As we are delivered from the bondage of false labels, we can walk in the freedom of believing what God speaks. When we believe what God speaks, we can move forward to walking in step with the Holy Spirit by believing the truth. After we have been released from the entanglement of false labels, we can step into more of what God is calling us to believe and declare. To do this, we have to meditate on His word so it gets inside of our hearts. Once it is in our hearts, we are able to boldly declare it to others without being ashamed of the gospel. When we boldly declare the gospel by believing what God speaks, we are bound to have people come against the truth. But we can remain firm in what God has spoken because we know His word proves true.

We have to decide whether or not we believe what God says. There is a difference between believing in God and believing—God. Believing in God is having faith in God. Believing—God is knowing He is trustworthy. That what He says will be fulfilled in due time. When we believe in God, we have faith that He is good. Whereas, believing—God, we are trusting what God says is true. We begin to believe that He speaks to us, and we learn to see the battle for belief vs unbelief. It is a battle for belief God speaks within our minds. This decision in our waiting journeys is a character development where God expands our faith to believe in the impossible. This establishment of our character growth in waiting is about whether or not we will keep choosing to believe what God speaks over what everyone else says. This goes back to knowing our identity is in Christ. By knowing we are a child of God, we have a firm foundation of our identity and who we are. When we know these things, it gets easier to believe God speaks to us. In knowing who we are in Christ, we can believe God and follow Him even if, to the world, we look like a fool.

Reflection questions:

What are some false labels you are facing?

How are you pouring out to be poured into?

What beliefs are you believing about yourself that are true or untrue?

What kind of waiting season are you in?

illuminated while waiting

What are you waiting for?

What are some tangible ways you can align your view of yourself with God's view of you?

Chapter Four

Believing God & Looking Like A Fool

Have you ever struggled to take God at His Word?

Has God ever asked you to do something that appeared foolish?

There was a time when I found it hard to take God at His Word. I thought it was completely foolish to keep praying and showing unconditional love to the man who broke my heart. I truly thought God was nuts for asking me to do this and foolish to show love to someone who had rejected me. But God's plan is far greater than mine. God showed me how doing what seems foolish to the world is rewarding to Him alone. Taking God at His Word meant setting aside my indifference to be obedient. He unveiled to me how showing unconditional love opens the door for restoration to take place in whatever way God deems necessary.

Believing God enough to willingly look like a fool takes faith in His living, active word. It takes trusting God enough not to care if we look foolish to others. This means being eager to stand our ground by remaining firm in what God has spoken over us. God conveyed this revelation by showing me how looking like a fool is okay and what His Word says is more precious than people's perception of me. Through my experience of sharing what the Lord spoke over me, I learned I needed to be prepared for criticisms from a few people and be ready to brush them off quickly and not dwell. I decided not to let what other people said create fear of how things looked; instead, I needed to pursue God's will. This is where I had to get out of my own way and allow God to remove those fears deep inside of my heart, to be flushed out and free from them.

The world will ridicule you for believing what God says. People will call you a liar and judge you in every single way possible. Sometimes they will even reject you for what you say or proclaim about God, and they will try to get you to doubt what God speaks over you. I have been ridiculed for believing what God spoke over me because it has not come to pass. When this arises, you have to choose to let go of the criticism.

Remember, Jesus does not reject you or toss you away. Instead, He pulls you close. Jesus has chosen you and created you for a purpose; He wants you to take Him at His Word. You are loved by God, and He does not forsake you nor will ever lie to you, because He cannot lie. You are made worthy through Christ and He is equipping you to step into your calling. Don't forget, God cannot be unfaithful to us because He is faithful and cannot go against His own character.

Your bold faith in God might appear silly to some, but you must stand firm and not allow their words or actions to shake you from the truth. Making the choice to take God at His Word means being willing to forsake everything to follow Him. It is taking up your cross, following hard after God with diligent faith, and letting go of all sin. Walking with God is counter-cultural. Believing God over circumstances takes grit, so we must remain firm and not let go of our faith. We must have a deep resolve not to back down when we encounter opposition. Unbelief cannot take root in our hearts. Grit to stand firm in faith is like a game of tug of war, but instead of giving up, we dig our heels in to win the game and prevail. Most often, when people think of grit, they think of sand. The grit I am referring to is having a posture and determination in our faith so as not to back down from what God has spoken over our lives.

As mentioned in the previous chapter, this even means tossing out the lies the enemy throws at us. Taking God at His Word helps us recognize the lies from people close to us and remove them from our minds so they do not take root. Once we believe in Him above all else, those who have been beside us could fall away or take the road more traveled instead of the road less traveled with God, who asks us to willingly choose to follow Him.

I have had many people who have tried to dissuade me from standing firm in God's truth. Yet, I had a choice to believe or walk away from God's promises. It became a very lonely place, walking down the road less traveled and taking God at His Word. Since other people did not experience what God spoke, it can be hard for them to understand, and they even tried to dissuade me from believing God's spoken Word. Without meaning to, they were attempting to plant a seed of doubt instead of just being there to listen. There are times family and friends can be good listeners in waiting seasons to lift us up when we are discouraged, but sometimes they need to hold their thoughts to themselves instead of sharing. I remember one instance when I was confiding to a friend about a situation, and instead of taking me at my word, she jumped to a different conclusion instead of seeking the truth. She twisted everything I was saying and completely misunderstood the situation. This is where we need to be careful and use discernment with whom we share and when we share. We must seek guidance from the Holy Spirit on whether to share or hold back.

The point is, we have to be okay with looking like fools for following God. He does not care about status, followers, posts, or fame. God cares about if we are open and willing to receive what He is speaking over us. Following and being obedient to God is more important than being surrounded by shallow things. This world is full of temporary possessions, but God is eternal.

> *But the LORD said to Samuel, "Do not look on his appearance or on the height of his stature, because I have rejected him. For the LORD sees not as man sees; man looks on the outward appearance, but the LORD looks on the heart.*
> 1 Samuel 16:7, ESV

In all honesty, I have been in the place of looking foolish to others by believing what God has spoken over me. Sometimes, I still look foolish to some people because I do not doubt what He has said to me. There are times when I can relate to Job in how he remained faithful to God and did not curse Him but remained steadfast. Job had moments when he went through so much and lost everything, but He did learn that God rewarded his steadfast faith in the end. This is where being careful in sharing what God spoke over us with others is important. Some things are meant for just us and Jesus. If God leads us to share with friends, the Holy Spirit will show us. It becomes a learning process of using discernment in each conversation we have. Job's friends didn't always stand by him and encourage him to remain faithful to God when they questioned God's goodness in Job's suffering. Job had to step back and remember God's faithfulness to be able to stand firm in knowing God's goodness and proclaim it. Job had to recognize God's goodness over the opinions of his friends and even his wife in order to withstand the shifting he was going through to not curse God and die.

Greater Faith To Take God At His Word

Greater faith to take God at His Word involves trusting that God calls things into existence that are not here yet. In following God and being willing to look foolish, we choose to believe Him, even if the promises He's given us do not happen in our lifetime... Sometimes waiting for God's promises takes years. In Genesis, we see how Noah was ridiculed for building the ark in a place where rain was never seen before. Noah believed God when He told him to build the Ark, even though people thought he was crazy (Genesis 6-8). But God proved faithful and flooded the earth showing Noah was not crazy, just obedient. Looking foolish is something we have to accept.

Holding steady in the promise God has spoken to us, requires faith and grit to see the hope in what He speaks, even when it does not immediately come to pass. We have to take hold of God's Word and know the promise is realized through our belief. Our faith in God must be greater than any doubt we may face. We must believe that God is a greater reward than anything on this earth will ever be, and the words He speaks are sweeter than anything on this earth.

> *That is why it depends on faith, in order that the promise may rest on grace and be guaranteed to all his offspring—not only to the adherent of the law but also to the one who shares the faith of Abraham, who is the father of us all, as it is written, "I have*

> *made you the father of many nations"—in the presence of the God in whom he believed, who gives life to the dead and calls into existence the things that do not exist. In hope he believed against hope, that he should become the father of many nations, as he had been told, So shall your offspring be."*
> Romans 4:16-18 ESV

Jesus is our sweet reward. He is our cornerstone who calls the dead things in us back to life. He is the one who gives us an abundance of blessings when we rest in His promises. The more we take God at His Word through our greater faith, the less fear will scare us. We can overcome anxiety and fear when we let go of our appearances and worries about others' opinions and be freed from the stronghold of fear. We must pick up our crosses daily to follow Jesus. Once we release our fears and doubts, we can cling to the certainty of the living, active word of God. Our fears no longer paralyze us. We can do this practically by journaling our fears to God. By writing prayers and scriptures down, we are actively taking God at His Word. In taking these fears to God, we put them back into His hands, and He takes the anxious burden off our shoulders. Another practical step in releasing our fears is saying what we are afraid of out loud to God. This takes the power of the fear out of us, realizing it does not control us since God is greater and His spirit is in us. Learning these strategies to take God at His Word helped me to remain firm in the truth to wait. Let me break it down for you;

Strategies:
1. Write down your fears.
2. Pray for God to release you from these fears.
3. Ask God to reveal anything that might be hindering you from taking God at His Word.

4. Quit hiding and find the confidence to speak out in obedience to God.

Being equipped with these strategies gave me the courage to step out in faith and helped me to stop being controlled by fear. God began to reveal to me I could not both hold onto fear and step into taking Him at His word. Fear and taking God at His word cannot co-exist; we have to choose one or the other. We are either led by fear or we are rooted in the truth of God. For example, because of being wounded by people, I was afraid to sing on any worship team no matter what church I attended. This was linked to my fear of the unknown and what could happen, even though I knew I was stronger than before. I was afraid of taking God at His word that said He had equipped me to do it. That fear of the unknown can cripple us into thinking we cannot do things God has called us to do. See, God calls us to believe without knowing all the details so we can learn to trust Him, despite unknowns that may be looming around.

Taking God at His word is believing what He says without signs, wonders, or miracles, and simply trusting His authority. It is blindly believing without seeing. In John 4:46-54, we see Jesus heal an official's son who is sick and dying. The interesting part of the passage is that Jesus does not run to the child's bedside but points out that the official wanted signs and wonders to believe Jesus could heal his son.

So he came again to Cana in Galilee, where he had made the water wine. And at Capernaum there was an official whose son was ill. When this man heard that Jesus had come from Judea to Galilee, he went to him and asked him to come down and heal his son, for he was at the point of death. So Jesus said to him, "Unless you see signs and wonders you will not believe." The official said to him, "Sir, come down before my

child dies." Jesus said to him, "Go; your son will live." The man believed the word that Jesus spoke to him and went on his way. As he was going down, his servants met him and told him that his son was recovering. So he asked them the hour when he began to get better, and they said to him, "Yesterday at the seventh hour the fever left him." The father knew that was the hour when Jesus had said to him, " Your son will live." And he himself believed, and all his household. This was now the second sign that Jesus did when he had come from Judea to Galilee.
John 4:46-54 ESV

Jesus healed the sick child not by publicly displaying a miracle, but by the power and authority of His spoken word. This was a prominent miracle of Jesus' words to allow people the opportunity to take Him at His word. What I learned is God has given us the authority and power to take Him at His word. It's quite astonishing to me how powerful His spoken words are to us and to everyone who believes. If we would take God at His word more often, we would be less stressed out and worried about life's unknowns. And we would not be so anxious about not having all the details laid out before us. It would be the same for me returning to sing again on a worship team because I know my voice and my strength level. I know worship is stronger where more than one is gathered. I know my voice will be weaker by myself than with someone else besides me. Being in isolation puts us in a weaker position to believe a lie over truth. That is exactly what Satan wants, us isolated so he can attack us in our weakest point. Fellowship and community with believers is important because we are stronger together. Even though there is the fear of the unknown, I must face my fears, but I do not have to face them alone because God is with me. I just have to remember the words God spoke over me and not doubt them; I don't want to fall into the trap of the sin of unbelief. It requires greater faith to take God at His word.

Taking God At His Word

By taking God at His word, we need to remember God does not make mistakes or mix up His words. He wants us to believe in Him. When we grab a hold of His word, we take steps to be a light for others. God speaks with intention and with excellence, shedding light on the dark places inside our hearts. He brings forth the good things within our hearts by encouraging us to step out into faith in the waiting seasons, but He also exposes the sin and lies we've been holding onto so we can fully embrace the truth. If we hold onto sin, lies, false labels, or fears, we will remain stuck in a cycle we will not want to be in. Stepping out in faith, we are taking a step outside of the dark into the light. By realizing a lie is holding us captive, we can walk free through faith in God's light.

I have learned and thrived in taking God at His word. My confidence in my identity in Christ has increased in what God speaks and in His love for me. It is not twisted or negative but based on the truth. My relationship with God has grown, and I have learned that speaking out in obedience is a form of taking God at His Word. I remember co-leading a women's Bible study and one thing God made clear to me was that He would equip me with the words to share. He made it abundantly clear I had to speak up because another woman's freedom was tied to the words God was giving me. God increased my confidence to get up and share what He put on my heart and not be afraid to speak out His words of healing. Another specific example of taking God at His word is that I had to trust how He was leading me to write this book. In the beginning, I had no idea how to begin. I was lost on where to start. But God gave me the words to write and the inspiration to do it. The takeaway from this: I had to be obedient in taking Him at His word and believe He'd give me the exact words that needed to be shared. I have found trusting God is worthwhile.

God does not go back on His Word or Promises but fulfills them in His timing.

Most importantly, I have learned that taking God at His word requires obedience and follow-through. Obedience is a word people often dislike as much as the word submit. However, to follow God, we must humble ourselves by believing through faith and obeying His commands. Obedience and follow-through are high on God's priorities—just as much as belief. Besides, when we take God at His word and hold fast to it, then, in a loving manner, we can rebuke those who contradict the truth:

> *He must hold firm to the trustworthy word as taught,*
> *so that he may be able to give instruction in sound*
> *doctrine and also to rebuke those who contradict it.*
> Titus 1:9 ESV

In this passage, Paul gives Titus instructions for what qualifies a person to be an elder. One of the things Paul points out in his letter to Titus is they need to hold fast to the truth to be able to rebuke contradictions against the truth. This portion of scripture is a reflection of Paul instructing Titus to take him at his word. It is the same between us and God. Speaking truth in love applies to us because we need not only to know the truth, but we also need to cling to it by remaining grounded in God's words.

Think about the process of training a horse. The trainer shows the horse time and again that they are trustworthy. This creates confidence in the horse that it can trust the trainer, the trainer won't harm it, and the horse can face new challenges. This partnership of trust is similar to our relationship with God. God has proven Himself faithful time and again. He will not lead us in the wrong direction but will lead us into all truth. We can partner with God because He has proven Himself faithful and we have assurance in our relationship with Him. In building a connection and relationship with your horse, you are creating a safe place of protection. In taking God at His word, we come to a place of trust in our relationship with God's word, where deep in our hearts, His spoken words can be trusted completely. We must know beyond a shadow of a doubt that God will not mislead us. He knows the way home.

Following God and believing the truth means forsaking all other things and holding close to the word of God. It is also about relying on the trust you have built in your relationship with Him. When we rely on this trust and connection, we are more willing to take God at His word because nothing can stand up to it. In this place of trust, we are able to discern whether or not what we believe is true. Once we can discern and rely on what is true, we can remember His character is always loving and good. Remembering God's good character is intertwined with taking Him at His word. Choosing to reflect on the goodness of God's character is a choice to not allow the disappointments that come in life cause us to stumble in believing God. It becomes a choice to firmly plant yourself in the assurance God has already given you.

When we base decisions on God's character and take Him at His word, we choose to live a life sold out to glorify our Father in heaven. It is in this place of humility and obedience where

God takes our faith to new levels and we step out in trust to take Him at His word. We did not come to trust men on this Earth, but we are here to trust, serve, and love God.

How can we learn to take God at His word? The first step is to discern if we believe the truth or if our beliefs are based on opinions. Next, we must determine whether or not we have heard from God in prayer, and ask the Holy Spirit to reveal if what we have heard aligns back to Scripture. Putting it simply, we must test what we hear with the truth. We must see if it is a reflection of God's good character. If it is, then we can take it as God's word.

Then, we look for confirmation of that word through Scripture, prayer, and sound counsel. Confirmations can come in simple or small ways, like a conversation with a friend, a message at church, or in a dream. Stand firm in the quiet confirmations God gives you.

Even if what God has spoken over you has not come to pass, His Word still stands.

Unexpected Blessing

Have you ever had God bring an unexpected blessing into your life?

God has a way of bringing things into our lives we could have never imagined. What I have learned in waiting is God works in many different ways. He brings us unexpected blessings as we learn to take Him at His Word. Don't limit how God speaks to you or how He brings confirmation of what He speaks. God does the unexpected in unexpected places with underestimated people who fulfill His glorious plans. Once in 2007, He used unexpected people to come into my life to bring a part of His glorious plan to fulfillment. We were moving back to Michigan after being in Tennessee for a while; a time of deep uncertainty for my family. God brought this amazing friend into my life who I did not expect— someone I could confide in and share things with that I've never felt safe sharing with others. This friend has been in my life for over fifteen years and is still someone I can talk to for prayer or anything. This friend whom God brought me was worth waiting for, and I did not even know I needed this person in my life. This friend is an unexpected safe place of protection, someone I can depend on and run to when I am scared, even if I annoy them at times. My friend is an unexpected gift I did not know I always wanted by my side. If I had turned down my friend's invitation to church that one day standing in the driveway of my new home where we met, I would have missed out on this astounding steadfast friend. It is a reminder of not only God's timing, but His glorious, unexpected blessings. I walked away knowing if I had not trusted God and taken Him at His Word in this situation, I would miss the blessing of this special friendship.

I love how God speaks in unexpected ways, revealing the truth we need to hear and bring people into our lives that we need. God moves through the Holy Spirit in fresh moments when we need it. He proceeds in ways with unexpected blessings to draw us closer, even taking a heart of stone to make it good soil. He will work in different ways throughout our lives to display His glorious grace in shifting our hearts. God moves with a fresh wind from the Holy Spirit to bring unexpected blessings we did not see coming. He will not always move in the same way; this is what makes God so good. He advances in ways we cannot predict to keep our hearts tender towards the unexpected blessings He places in our lives. We need God to speak to our hearts in different ways, so we can receive it at the right time. Sometimes God brings unexpected people into our lives to speak the truth over us that we were not sure we needed to hear.

I always say to expect the unexpected from God because He moves the impossible; we just need faith to believe it. God takes what appears impossible to us and makes it possible through Him alone. It is astonishing how God takes the simple things to make them unexpected blessings in our lives. Our faith in God can move mountains; we just have to believe that God is actually telling the truth.

> *Every word of God proves true; he is a shield to those*
> *who take refuge in him. Do not add to his words,*
> *lest he rebuke you and you be found a liar.*
> *Proverbs 30:5 ESV*

God never fails. He always moves behind the scenes even when we cannot see the evidence. His fingerprints are not always seen, but His love can always be seen even in unexpected ways. Therefore, we cannot limit God or put Him in a box. If we try to track every single move God makes, we will become exhausted because He moves in ways we can't predict, beyond our expectations and comprehension. God has already won the victory. He has defeated death through the death and resurrection of His son Jesus Christ. He has the power to move in unexpected ways full of blessings because God has won the battle.

Since God is trustworthy, we do not have to worry about what comes next. He is already working on our behalf in the waiting seasons. God is moving into the place of the next unexpected blessing for us, we just have to accept it when it comes. We have assurance God is trustworthy and He will work all things together for our good (Romans 8:28). It all goes back to believing God and being willing to look like a fool even if the world is laughing at you.

We need to understand and believe that God does not go back on His Word. He is always faithful; even in the trials and struggles, He is there. God will not leave us alone when He calls us to step out in faith. Believing God in the waiting season takes faith to stand out when it looks like you are standing alone. But we can rest in Jesus because we know He is already doing the unexpected for us.

In seasons of waiting, there are times when God calls us out in simple obedience so a miracle can occur for a breakthrough to come to pass, which is usually attached to the promise He has already spoken over us. In waiting, we still have to follow God's lead, not our selfish ways. But let me remind you, the simple things we do for God are small miracle glimpses of hope to keep us going in the waiting. The unexpected blessings from God come at times we are not looking for them. These blessings are a manifestation of the bigger blessings He is bringing into our lives.

Waiting does not have to be dull or dreary. Waiting seasons are full of unpredicted blessings from God. It is a time of preparation for our hearts to be ready for the anointing that is to come. If we are not ready or spiritually mature to take on what God is calling us to do, we could flounder instead of flourish. While waiting, we learn to believe God for His unexpected favor despite what the world thinks. God teaches us to release things into His hands to grab hold of His unexpected blessings while we wait. As mentioned in previous chapters, He helps us see the light and expose the lies we have believed in the past. We also learn how to recognize His voice, allowing us to remain firm in our faith because we know God's Word is trustworthy.

Waiting seasons unveil how the goodness of God is so faithful, even when we do not see the evidence of what He has spoken over us. God remains steadfast, continuing to show us that believing for His unanticipated blessing is more beneficial than what the world offers. A reminder of the goodness of God is tied to believing what He says is worth looking foolish to the world. God's goodness is also intertwined with His unexpected blessings in the way He brings people into our lives to bless us. The unexpected blessing of the friend God brought into my life has been abundantly more than I could ever imagine. God even brings me encouraging messages when I need them from unexpected places. I will share a quote from the very message from Pastor Jason Rollin of City Light Church and his sermon that encouraged me not to give up on the promise called *"In Between the Pain and the Promise."* He said,

> *"Don't give up on the waiting. We war consistently. We war with confidence."* [4]

During waiting seasons, God speaks to the dark places in our hearts to bring them to light so we can see His unforeseen blessings in the relationships–friends He brings into our lives. He exposes fears that from out of hiding we are too afraid to face by purifying our hearts to war with confidence in faith. The way God so lovingly brings the dark places in our hearts to light does not shame us. I love seeing God's handiwork in the waiting. He removes the fear of giving up and frees us from it. What is wise in the world's eyes is foolish to God, and what is wise to God is unwise to the world's standards. There is a greater reward in warring with God and looking like a fool to the world. The greater reward is the unexpected blessings that come out of believing God and what He pours out on you through the waiting seasons you go through.

> *For the wisdom of this world is folly with God...*
> 1 Corinthians 3:19a ESV

In my journey of waiting, God has called me out to believe Him while looking like a fool to those around me. He does not make me feel ashamed of believing in His spoken word. Instead, God continues to give me blessings and affirmations while I wait for His best. Even when people around me call me foolish or say things to discourage me in the waiting, God confirms that His word is coming to pass through answered prayers. He is gracious enough to show me He hears my prayers.

> *Then he said to me, "Fear not, Daniel, for from the first day that you set your heart to understand and humbled yourself before your God, your words have been heard, and I have come because of your words. The prince of the kingdom of Persia withstood me twenty-one days, but Michael, one of the chief princes, came to help me, for I was left there with the kings of Persia, and came to make you understand what is to happen to your people in the latter days. For the vision is for days yet to come."*
> Daniel 10:12-14 ESV

Therefore, when you feel discouraged about what you are waiting for or who you are waiting for, go back to the spoken word and promise God has given you. Remember, His word still stands. Dig into God's Word to find more confirmations and give your heart peace. Ask and seek God for a fresh awakening so you do not turn away or give up on His promises. God loves to pour out and lavish us with His unending peace. God also loves to commune with us because of our relationship with Him. Remember, when we seek God, we will find Him and know Him. He is a personal God who speaks in love. There are so many confirmations God has given me about what He has spoken over me; I cannot begin to count them. They are so vast and deep. I challenge you to write down the things God has promised you and make a list of the things God is calling you to war with Him confidently.

Reflection Questions:

How has God called you out to look like a fool for Him?

What fear is holding you back from stepping out in faith?

What are some unexpected blessings God is showing you?

How can you have the grit to take God at His Word?

Chapter Five

The Good Shepherd

Has there ever been a time when you had a hard time recognizing God's voice?

Recognizing God's voice is not hard to do. We must be willing to listen and receive what He says. There comes a point where we just need to give up and say, "Okay, I am listening to you, God." He wants us to be familiar with His voice. God speaks in unexpected ways, but as His children, we learn to know and recognize His voice. We follow God because we know He is good and won't mislead us. He is the Good Shepherd who leads us in truth, even when we mess up and sin or when we choose to grab temporary things that are a substitute instead of waiting on God. He gives us a heart to discern His voice because He loves us. God created us to shepherd us.

> *I will give them a heart to know that I am the LORD,*
> *and they shall be my people and I will be their God,*
> *for they shall return to me with their whole heart.*
> Jeremiah 24:7 ESV

In this passage, Jeremiah is given a word from the Lord about the exiles in Judah, comparing them to good figs and bad figs. Jeremiah refers to these exiles being brought back because they are God's chosen people who recognize He is their shepherd. God wants all of us to discern His voice even when we fall short. There was a time when I was having a hard time being conscious of God's voice. I was trying to make things happen instead of resting in Jesus and allowing Him to lead and speak to me. During this time I was ignoring where He was leading me to go. When we jump ahead of God's timing to force things to happen or manipulate to get people to do what we want, it blows up in our faces. This revelation of light was unveiled to me when I tried going ahead of God. When I first started looking at colleges, I tried looking at traditional options and all different kinds of avenues instead of stepping into and seeking what God thought on the matter first. Everything was in a tizzy because nothing was falling into place. It was not until I stopped and asked God for help did the avenue of Bible College come into focus and fall into place. I had to slow down and pray to be led by God. I had to stop leading myself in order to be led by the Good Shepherd. I learned by following God's lead that the doors that open while waiting are full of more blessings than the ones we try to force open ourselves. I released my unrealistic expectations of what I thought should happen into God's hands.

When we wait on God's timing and let Him go ahead of us like a good shepherd who loves His sheep, we gain understanding and wisdom to know He will work things out for our good. The knowledge we receive helps us be aware of God's voice to follow Him. But it comes back to trusting God with the unknowns; we already know He is completely capable. Within the gospel of John, we see Jesus lay out a foundation of how He is a Good Shepherd and how He loves us enough to lay down His life for us (John 10:11).

The religious Jews asked Jesus to tell them plainly who He was, but Jesus had already told them by saying He was the Good

The Good Shepherd

Shepherd. Do you find it interesting how the Jewish people and religious leaders did not believe Jesus when He came to fulfill Scripture and the Jewish Law? I find it astounding how Jesus spoke to those who did not believe. These people did not recognize His voice because they were lost. Not only did they not believe Jesus, but they did not trust what He spoke. In this chapter, Jesus explains how a flock of sheep will only recognize their shepherd's voice and will flee from strangers.

Jesus also reveals to us in this chapter that a good shepherd will lay down His life for His sheep, yet a stranger or a thief would not protect the sheep but would let them wander off. We need to take this approach in learning how to discern when listening to someone besides God. We must flee from the lies of the enemy and anyone who speaks lies. We need to turn our attention to the Word of God when the enemy tries to attack us with untruth.

Let me encourage you. Jesus does not walk away from His sheep, and nothing can snatch us out of His hand once we belong to Him (John 10:27-28). Jesus' voice cannot be mistaken by His sheep because He is known by them. There is a trust factor between a shepherd and his sheep. Jesus will never hide His voice from His sheep because they can always recognize Him. In recognizing Jesus' voice, we are led into all truth, and in learning this, the lies of the enemy cannot stand against it. When Jesus speaks to us, we are led away from lies by being equipped with the truth. When we speak out the truth, the enemy flees. As I was armed with these strategies of knowing and recognizing Jesus as my shepherd, I began to want others to know Jesus as their Shepherd, too.

Strategies:
1. Ask Jesus to help you recognize His voice.
2. Pray for Jesus to reveal the blessings of recognizing His voice.
3. Ask the Lord to help you if you feel lost.
4. Seek Jesus and ask Him to reveal what the enemy is trying to steal.
5. Speak the Word of God out loud.

Having these strategies helped me to understand Jesus as my shepherd. These strategies gave me a glimpse of how Jesus is gentle in how He leads us to know we are not lost sheep in the wilderness. In reading John 10, I also realized that as Jesus was sharing how He was the Good Shepherd, some people did not believe what He said to them. If the Jews themselves were sheep, they would flee because the things Jesus was saying turned the tables on everything they knew about their laws and customs. See, sheep follow the shepherd because they know His voice and recognize who He is. I have heard many different pastors and spiritual leaders throughout my life say sheep are dumb. Yet, I would beg to differ. Sheep will always flee from a stranger's voice and run to the protection of the shepherd. They are smarter than we realize or give them credit for. If sheep only follow the shepherd because they know the shepherd's voice and trust that he will protect them, then sheep must be smart enough to recognize their shepherd's voice. If you grew up like me, your parents told you about "stranger danger" and told you not to talk with strangers. Meaning, they informed you to flee from a stranger's voice. It is the same for us when God instructs us to follow what He says instead of listening to the enemy. Sometimes, we fall short by acting like the Pharisees, not listening to Jesus shepherd us. The religious leaders during Jesus' time on Earth could not recognize that He was the Son of God. This points out how they could not be

The Good Shepherd

sheep because they could not recognize Jesus, the Shepherd's voice. These religious leaders could not discern that Jesus was the Messiah, the Son of God. They were too blinded by how Jesus broke religious rules to heal people and lead them in truth.

What's interesting about the sheep in John 10 is that those who know the good shepherd's voice are obedient to respond because of the trust between them. This is exactly the kind of trust we need to have in our relationship with Christ—blind faith in Jesus because He will not mislead us or harm us. Instead, Christ does things for our good, even when those things are unseen. Jesus is still the Good Shepherd and always will be.

I am the good shepherd, and I know my own and my own know me, just as the Father knows me and I know the Father, and I lay down my life for the sheep. And I have other sheep that are not of this fold. I must bring them also, and they will listen to my voice. So there will be one flock, one shepherd.
John 10:14-16 ESV

As I was poring over this chapter, it became clear that Jesus not only lays down His own life for us as the Good Shepherd, but He also knows us, and we know Him. His voice is distinct and recognizable to us, so we can know Jesus intimately and draw close without hesitation. Jesus does not hide His voice but speaks to us plainly until we grasp it. It is a relief to know God does not invoke suffering upon us because that is outside of His good character. God is a good Father who goes before us to lead the way, never leaving us alone. I remember a long time ago when I felt alone, but God showed me He is my good shepherd. When I was a little girl, I went on a skiing field trip with my mom and my brother at a nearby ski area with a group of homeschoolers. My mom wasn't able to ski on this trip, so she remained in the lodge while we went out . . . to say I was a little scared is an understatement. We began skiing together as a group, but somehow one of my skis got stuck in the snow, leaving me behind. Everyone kept going on the ski trail, including my brother, but one little boy I did not know came upon me when I was lost and stayed with me until someone would come back to find me. After the group got back to the lodge without me, the leaders said they would not go back out to look for me, which made my mom feel both furious and helpless. My brother decided to go back out on the ski trail to look for me. As he was looking for me, he began calling out my name. The closer he got, I was able to identify his voice. My brother's voice became recognizable, almost like he was a shepherd boy looking for his sheep. He found me where I was lost in the wilderness and led me back to safety. This story reminded me how God is my Good Shepherd, in how He used my brother to go look for the one lost sheep. I was the lost sheep, but God knew where I was the whole time and kept me safe despite my fears.

I love how when Jesus speaks, He speaks up to silence the enemy.

Recognizing His Voice

The people who believed and followed Jesus were able to discern He was the Son of God, the Messiah, because they were sheep who recognized He was the Good Shepherd. A true and good shepherd like Jesus carries His sheep when they stumble or cannot find their way. Jesus came to reveal the truth and lead us into truth to be saved. As John MacArthur says in *The MacArthur Bible Commentary*, *"In [John] chapter 10,*

The Good Shepherd

Jesus declared Himself to be the "Good Shepherd" who was appointed by His Father as Savior and King, in contrast to the false shepherds of Israel who were self-appointed and self-righteous (Ps 32:1, Is 40:11. Jer.3:15; cf, Is 56:9-12; Jer.23:1-4; 25:32-38, Ezek,34:1-31;Zech.11:16)." [5]

In John 10, Jesus gave a metaphor of how He will not mislead people, like how the people of Israel were being led astray by false shepherds. These can also be called false teachers who mislead people away from God. This is a display of how God wants us to acknowledge He will always lead us in truth. It astounds me how vast and wide God's love goes as our Good Shepherd, and it can be seen in the verses *John MacArthur* gives within the quote I shared above. In Jesus, we are one flock united in the love of God and the Holy Spirit. We are united through the work Jesus did on the cross and resurrection to discern His voice. He is the only shepherd of truth and light. Everything else fails and falls short of the glory of God. Doesn't that just give you abundant peace in knowing we have a savior and shepherd who does not fail to protect or love us? God is not far away from us but is always at our side. God does not ignore us in the waiting but gives us room to voice our deepest prayers within our hearts. God leads us through waiting seasons to be refreshed with hope to keep expectation of what God is doing.

Some days, that truth just takes my breath away. Romans 8 is a good reminder of how nothing can separate us from the love of God or can snatch us out of the hand of Christ. It is also a reminder that God does not mislead us but always takes us in the right direction. In the waiting times of life, we need to be led instead of taking the lead. To do this we have to step back and listen for God's voice, identify it, and follow Him. We do not have all the details, and when we jump ahead of God's leading, we create a cheap substitute for God's best for us. I don't know about you, but I want to experience God's best, His rich and abundant blessings. I want to know and recognize His voice above all.

Blessings To Recognizing God's Voice

One of the greatest blessings in waiting for God's best is getting to know Jesus more. A beautiful expression of love is how God gives us more of Himself in our waiting. Another is getting to the point in our relationship with God that we can be completely honest with Him. Honesty frees us from the bondage of sin, which can be connected to any kind of shame we have experienced. Being honest with God helps to lay out all of our fears before His throne so we can be ready for the next thing or person He puts before us. Falling more in love with Jesus is a fun journey that never ends. There is always something new to learn about Jesus and learning to hear His voice.

If we are holding onto things that have hurt us in the past, we may not be ready to embrace what God has for us. Forgiveness is a blessing of learning to identify God's voice as you wait. It is a blessing because forgiveness is a step to healing our hearts. Pardoning what has been done to us or spoken over us is allowing the blessing of God's love to replace bitterness with peace. This is where forgiveness is key in letting go of anything holding us back from embracing honesty in our relationship with God. Another blessing in waiting is being in constant prayer over what or who we are waiting for God to bring into our lives. Continuing to pray over it releases it from our hands, puts it back into God's, and gives us peace. We can rest in the presence of God, knowing it is covered. Constant

The Good Shepherd

prayer opens the door to hear God's voice clearly.

Resting in the presence of God is a blessing that gives us the strength to be grounded in following Jesus' leading. Slowing down to be in God's presence allows us to enjoy hearing God's voice. Standing firm to believe what God has spoken over us is half the battle in waiting for things to come to pass. It is having the foolish faith to not give up by following Jesus' lead. Choosing faith over facts is part of learning to follow Jesus, the Good Shepherd. All of us will be faced with the choice to follow the good shepherd or follow our own foolish ways of the flesh, whether we are single, newly married, a new mom, expanding family, or anything else. A determination to have faith in our messy circumstances of life is the same as choosing truth over believing a lie. We have to stand firm in faith to be able to follow Jesus, our Good Shepherd.

Seeing people through Jesus' lens is a blessing of learning to hear what God speaks over them. Jesus leads us to see people through His eyes as a shepherd of truth compared to our flawed views. Getting to see people through a different lens rather than our own helps us realize God wants His voice known by all His children. Besides, believing God in the waiting helps us gain a different perspective on life and how we are becoming who God has called us to be. Believing in God's spoken promises requires the strength to follow the Good Shepherd's leading we have never seen before. This will test our faith which we have established in having the grit to abide in our God the Good Shepherd. Also, it is a strength to rest in God's peace and know that God works things out for our good. Even when other people are involved, God is still in the situation, within our midst, going before us and leading the way for us to follow. This is something we must not forget.

The LORD has taken away the judgments against you; he has cleared away your enemies. The King of Israel, the LORD, is in your midst; you shall never again fear evil.
Zephaniah 3:15 ESV

While in our midst, God makes a way for us to recognize His voice. He clears away the obstacles and barriers, so He is the only thing that remains. God is with us in the good times and in the messy times. Even when we cannot walk, He carries us through. God does not leave us when we are hurting or broken. It is here where God speaks to us the loudest to hear His sweet grace pour into us. Those moments are when He captivates our hearts to focus on His unfailing love. It is also in those moments when God sweetly speaks over our hearts to quiet our minds, which can be loud with doubt. When God speaks to us, He speaks with authority, which is how we learn to know it is Him speaking to us and not anyone else. As I think about God as the Good Shepherd I remember how He led me to get involved in youth ministry during college, to serve the freshman girls at the large church connected to the Bible College I was attending. I had no intention of getting so involved, but He did. God kept speaking until I recognized He was nudging me to move in this direction. My focus in college was to keep my head in the books to get good grades. But God wanted me to pour into these high school girls so they would recognize God's voice in their own lives. During this time in college, my love for others to know Christ grew because God led me to serve in this capacity. After college, I began to get involved at the Bible church closer to home. At this church, the Pastor asked the congregation if anyone would want to teach a children's story before the kids got dismissed from service to go to the children's church. God led me to have the courage to volunteer to teach a children's story. I would have never done this on my own without the guidance of God. I was able to quickly discern God was asking me to volunteer for this.

In these sweet moments, when we remember God is in our midst, we are reminded the spoken promises of God are not empty but full of many blessings. We know there are blessings in His promises because God is our Shepherd, who leads us into truth. The closer we draw to God, the more we see the blessings of recognizing His voice as our shepherd; we then get the privilege of seeing more of His promises come to pass. He will not promise us something or speak something over us if it is not true. Let me remind you God will not condemn or shame His children for something they did or did not do. That is not how God works. God corrects in a loving way. He speaks and guides us in what is true. He shepherds us as a way to learn to identify His voice more distinctly. God does not hide His voice, and His promises are full of abundant blessings. Our Jesus has given us an inside look into how He shepherds us with gentleness. His tenderness in how He corrects us does not bring us shame but shows us how to step out in freedom. God wants us to experience and live in freedom, not bondage. This is why He shepherds us in truth. God speaks to us as our Shepherd and calls us to freedom. This is a blessing of being conscious of His voice. I love how He is not a bossy God but one full of mercy and grace. He has cleared judgments from us. God is in our midst. He has wiped away the past and forgiven us by giving us a clean slate. God does not keep a record of our wrongs to use against us. He has restored us to wholeness.

God is faithful in His love! God's promises remain true!

Reflection Questions:

How do you know if you are leading or if God is leading you?

illuminated while waiting

How can you discern God's voice?

What blessings can you see?

Chapter Six

Blessings in the Waiting

There are blessings in waiting, even if they are hard to see. We will see blessings by persevering and resting in Jesus. God shows us even when we least expect it. Persevering and not forcing things to happen requires knowing God does not go back on His word and His promises are never empty. He fulfills what He speaks over us in due time. Besides, when we believe with expectancy in the promises of God, there are abundant blessings that come with waiting for them. Forcing things prevents us from seeing the blessing of waiting. God's words are spoken with purpose and intention. His words of truth are never wasted but full of promises. God's blessings in the waiting began showing me how His promises are fulfilled in His time. He showed me these things in prayer, teaching me to remain faithful and to see hope while waiting. An expectant heart and attitude help us to see hidden blessings God has for us in our quiet time in prayer. As God answered small prayers and promises, I began to see more of His goodness to keep believing. I began to see the blessings of waiting through experiencing answered prayers.

Seeing prayers answered also helps us understand that even if something is outside our control, God still loves us. We do not have to force things. He is working it out for our good. God sees us and is not silent but moves behind the scenes in a way we cannot comprehend or even imagine. And when God moves, He brings people together to unite them through His love. In every kind of relationship here on Earth, God brings us together to glorify Him and be in a relationship with Him. God connects people in a similar way to how we are connected to Him. Also, God must be at the center of each relationship and friendship we have. When God is at the center, there is peace, unity, and love. I was listening to a sermon that a friend sent me by Robert Morris. It is called *"Finding Purpose in Waiting: Trusting God's Perfect Timing."* He said,

> *"You need to wait in a relationship with God and with God's people. Stay connected to God in the waiting with fervent prayer. The farther we get from prayer, the farther we get from receiving the continuous power and promise of the Holy Spirit."*[6]

These wise words from Robert Morris are a reminder of how important building a close relationship with God is. They are words prompting us to not forget to wait with fervent prayer and supplication to God. Going to God in prayer puts Him at the center and takes the burden off ourselves. Putting the burden back on God helps us to persevere and not force things to happen. When God is not the center of all our relationships or friendships, there can be strife and unforgiveness. In these situations, it is because manipulation or forcing things to happen was the center instead of giving God room to move. Most likely, hurt feelings end up in the mix, too. This is when anger and bitterness can fill our hearts instead of the agape love of God. The enemy likes to worm his way into our relationships and friendships to cause division and dissension to bring separation of God's kingdom. This can lead us to believe lies about God or what He has spoken to us. When God is the center, we wait with an assurance of the promise and allow perseverance to grow our character.

For still the vision awaits its appointed time; it hastens to the end—it will not lie. If it seems slow, wait for it; it will surely come; it will not delay.
Habakkuk 2:3 ESV

God's promises cannot be forced. They can only be received. The promises of God do not lie, and they are always fulfilled at the appointed time. God cannot go back on His promises. No one can undo what God says and speaks. God speaks with intention and diligence. He is not lazy but is fighting for us, and He is not far. Instead, He is close and is waiting with us so we can reach out to Him at any moment. Forcing things takes away the excitement and joy of seeing God move within our lives. God fulfills His promises in His timing and not ours. Even though we may think it is slow, this is not true because God's promises arrive exactly when we need them. God is always on time.

Not Forcing But Persevering

I want to emphasize that we cannot force things to happen. We cannot force people to do what we want, either. Trust me, I have tried, and it got me nothing except disappointment and misery. In doing this, we miss the blessings of waiting and learning to persevere. Trying to force things to happen, especially with relationships, can lead to hurt feelings or a broken heart. Manipulating things to happen can also lead to miscommunication and false assumptions.

Therefore, since we have been justified by faith, we have peace with God through our Lord Jesus Christ. Through him

> *we have also obtained access by faith into this grace in which we stand, and we rejoice in hope of the glory of God. Not only that, but we rejoice in our sufferings, knowing that suffering produces endurance, and endurance produces character, and character produces hope, and hope does not put us to shame, because God's love has been poured into our hearts through the Holy Spirit who has been given to us.*
> *Romans 5:1-5 ESV*

This passage revives our souls to see that perseverance produces hope and that hope will help us grow closer to God. It is also a reminder of how our character will be refined while persevering through life. Having the endurance to see God move in your life is a step of having faith, which can move mountains. Perseverance helps us to remain firm in faith because it is a form of grit–endurance to not give up. Forcing things is a substitute for emptiness and lacks substance. When we jump ahead of God and try to force things to happen or force things on people, we create an atmosphere of division for the enemy to steal, kill, and destroy what we are trying so badly to hold on to. The best thing we can do is go before the throne of Jesus and lay it all bare before His holy feet. Prayer in itself is a blessing because we are drawing closer in our relationship with Jesus. Through prayer, we can take these things burdening our hearts before God to pray over situations and people. Our character is growing further in faith by laying these burdens before His throne. By laying these burdens down, we can go deeper with our trust in God to not force things but rest in Jesus as we wait. We need to pray over these things instead of jumping ahead of the promise God has spoken over us. God does not withhold His promises but fulfills them. God is good, and His character never changes but remains the same. Thus, we must remember the promise will come to pass, yet we must wait and believe with an expectancy that will bring blessings of abundance.

> *And blessed is she who believed that there would be a fulfillment of what was spoken to her from the Lord.*
> Luke 1:45 ESV

Persevering and not forcing is resting in trusting the words God speaks over you. Letting perseverance have its work in us is surrendering to God. Yes, waiting can be hard, and it can be lonely. But waiting is worthwhile and full of abundant blessings. We can grow a deeper faith in God and stronger perseverance to trust Him. Waiting gives us the blessing of time with Jesus to align our hearts with Him before He brings other people into our lives, whether it is a friendship or a romantic relationship.

Waiting for God's spoken promises to come to pass develops perseverance and sanctification within us and our faith in God by seeing the waiting as a blessing, not an obstacle. We learn not to give in to believing the enemy's lies to forfeit God's spoken promises over us. We must stand our ground by learning that our grit factor is in our faith in God, not our circumstances. Our faith must be in Jesus, not in this world. We must have the resolve to keep believing in the promises of God. Seeing God put such an emphasis on having a deep grit in my faith made me want to keep these strategies of this resolve in the forefront of my mind. God also laid on my heart that more of His children needed to know these strategies so they could experience a deep grit of faith.

Strategies:
1. Pray for God to open your eyes to where you need grit.
2. Ask God to fill the lack of perseverance.
3. Seek God to have Him reveal where you are forcing things instead of resting.

I realize these strategies may sound simple. But they can be life-changing. Approach God with humility, seeking to gain a stronger faith in Him. The more we rest in Jesus instead of forcing things the easier the waiting gets.

Blessings of Friends While Persevering

Although waiting for the promises of God to come to pass is not always easy or full of sunshine, it is worthwhile in the end. It also gives us time with God to experience the blessings of bringing new friendships into our lives to help us grow in faith. He will restore and heal relationships and friendships that were broken. My journey has involved God bringing new friends into my life through more virtual places than face-to-face. This group of women are radiant warriors for Jesus. They are friends who I know have my back and will pray truth over every single situation we may face. These ladies will speak in tongues and declare God's authority over every circumstance. I am beyond grateful for these friends who encourage me and lift up my arms when I cannot hold them up myself. However, it has been an experience of refinement in iron sharpening iron (Proverbs 27:17), which encourages me to keep my confidence. These new friends have helped me remember God's faithfulness when I have been distracted. The new friendships have sharpened me as they pray for me and encourage me to dig deeper with God. I have had the opportunity to do the same for them.

Iron sharpens iron, and one man sharpens another.
Proverbs 27:17 ESV

We cannot hold onto the old and grab onto the new. There are friendships God will shut the door on to protect us, or that may be hindering us from learning not to force things. New friendships have helped me to grab onto the new things God was speaking to me. Thus, to grab ahold of the promises of God and the new things He puts into our lives, we have to let go of what is holding us back and move into what He has called us to do by simply being obedient to what He asks us to do next. We can do this when we have people around us and friends who will speak encouragement to us in truth.

Friends whom we have a deep relationship with can see things in us that we need to see or hear when we are waiting and help us discern if our hearts are in the right position. They are able to call things out in us that we are too afraid to admit to ourselves. There are times when friends are needed to give us a good push outside our comfort zones to fulfill the calling God has put on our lives. Don't get me wrong, friends in our lives cannot take the place of God. They are meant to help us draw closer to God and listen to the truth. They speak truth in love.

Listening To Persevere

Listening to God to persevere is more important than doing all the talking. It's not wrong to lay your burdens down before God, but we also need to listen to what He says. I realize that sometimes, as human beings, we can overcomplicate things by overthinking too much when we just need to step back, take a breath, be silent, and sit in the presence of God for a while. The point is, sometimes, we just need to be still and listen instead of always talking. Paying attention to persevere is taking what God is speaking to us and putting it into action rather than just complaining. It is taking what we hear in prayer with God and putting measures in place to do what God is telling us. Now, let me point out that most people who know me see the quiet part of me most of the time. Within my own prayer time, sometimes

I like to talk too much, sometimes out loud, sometimes in my head. I have learned I just need to be still to see the blessings of God in the waiting and how God's promises are never empty. Sometimes I just need to talk with a friend to gain perspective and talk things out to see God reveal His truth in a new way.

Other times, I find it more beneficial to listen rather than to speak to gain a better perspective on things. Hearing God speak His promises over me and waiting expectedly for them helped me be quick to listen and slow to speak. For perseverance to build our character, we must slow down and listen to the promptings of the Holy Spirit. This is when we take a stance of humility before God, putting ourselves in a position to hear God speak goodness over us. What this means is I had to position myself to hear God, and in doing this, I was able to persevere and not give up. My faith in God is what has kept me grounded to stand firm when everything around me was trying to convince me to disbelieve what God said.

Positioning ourselves to hear God takes intentionality to pursue what God speaks over us and realize God's promises are never empty. This is where we cannot let pride or anything else get in the way. If something clouds what we believe about God or what He has said over us, then we begin to doubt the credibility of God's promises. This means if we allow doubt to creep in, we allow unbelief to cloud our judgment of who God is, and then we will miss the blessings of waiting. But if we submit to God's authority, we can persevere to stand firm in faith. Being surrounded by a community of believers helps us to be refreshed in hearing God speak to us by sharing our experiences.

This is where humility before God helps us see God's promises are not empty but full of goodness. If we are not willing to be led by the Holy Spirit and God's leading, we will not be able to hear God's voice and see the blessings of perseverance and friendships that God gives in waiting. The enemy's lies will misconstrue what God has spoken to discount or get us to doubt his voice. God does not hide His promises from us but shares them with us. So we can anticipate them coming to pass and enjoy the blessings of those spoken promises. This is having confidence in God and His word, where nothing can dissuade us from believing what God has spoken.

Truth To Persevere

Through the process of waiting, we learn to rest in God's peace while persevering before the promises come to pass. We also learn to enjoy the presence of God more throughout the process. Waiting on God challenges us to persevere by fully relying on God instead of getting instant gratification as the world does. In the waiting, we have to stand our ground and not let what is happening around us or what is not happening cause us to give up or give in to believing lies.

While waiting, we need to be pressing into the presence of God to hear His voice more clearly. When we move in closer, His voice gets louder. In case that did not sink in, the more we persist in seeking God, the more we will know Him and His voice. The more we know God, the more we can rest in His presence to persevere in the waiting. Plus the more we rest in God's presence, the more we will be able to recognize God's voice because He wants to be known by us. Remember, God does not disguise His voice from us,. God wants to draw us closer, not push us away. God created us with a purpose to be in a relationship with us, not separated. That is why God redeemed us through the loving sacrifice of Jesus dying on the cross for us. God makes himself known to us because He loves us. God does not hide from us, which also means we should not hide from Him. God wants us to stand our ground in truth, and He wants us to lean in so we can know Him better.

And the word of the LORD came to me, saying, "Jeremiah, what do you see?" And I said, "I see an almond branch." Then the LORD said to me, "You have seen well, for I am watching over my word to perform it."
Jeremiah 1:11-12 ESV

I realize in the Christian culture it is said God's timing is perfect, because God does not mess up or make mistakes. Yet, the point that also needs to be made is God does not make empty promises or mislead us.

For example, God is like a compass: His word and truth always point to the true north. It never breaks down or points us in the wrong direction. It guides us into all truth through the work of the Holy Spirit to make us more holy and more like Christ. As we run to the Father to know the truth to persevere, we gain strength to keep faith in our journey. Being illuminated while waiting for God's promises is a journey of faith, and choosing to have confidence and persevere in God rather than the world. This world and culture have this fad going on where truth can be exchanged and changed constantly, and "my truth does not have to reflect your truth." This is completely silly. The truth does not change. It remains the same. Knowing the truth does not change is a blessing and gives us something to stand on. In the *Believer's Bible Commentary, William MacDonald* affirms how God's word is proven true and should not be added to. He says,

"The absolute sufficiency of the Scriptures is asserted next.

No man should dare to add his thoughts and speculations to what God has spoken. This verse condemns the cults which give their own writings and traditions the same authority as the Bible."[7]

The Word of God is truth; nothing can stand up against it. God's Word is living and active. It is sharper than a two-edged sword. Nothing can come against God's Word and disqualify it. People have tried, and some have even tried to misrepresent it, but it remains constant because it is God's script. There is a difference between opinions and the truth. People have opinions and make statements, which is fine, but God's Word burns true every single time.

"This God—his way is perfect; the word of the LORD proves true; he is a shield for all those who take refuge in him."
2 Samuel 22:31 ESV

Even after over two thousand years, it is still there. God's truth is fire; it will not only stand for itself, but it will burn on our lips to testify what is true and what is not. God's truth cannot contradict itself. The truth is everlasting. As people, we can have opinions where we contradict ourselves without realizing it by confusing *"my truth"* instead of *the* truth. Although we are limited finite human beings, we are in Christ, and we have the truth in us. God's spirit lives in us. We can know the truth, but we must go to the source to understand it.

We can have peace in knowing that God will lead us to persevere in our faith. Because the Spirit and truth are in us, we can rest in knowing He fulfills His promises. In the waiting seasons, we end up learning that God does not go back on His word. This does take time in learning how God remains faithful to His word. Sometimes it takes a while for us to realize how faithful

He is. When we realize God's faithfulness, we realize what a blessing it is to know God has our back no matter what.

God Helps You Persevere

We do not have to clean ourselves up before we run to Jesus. He takes us as we are, to cleanse us in making us more like Him. We can lay our mess before Jesus and let Him do work through us. He helps us persevere when we want to give up. God can handle our mess right away, but sometimes we are slow to learn this lesson. To do this we need to listen for God's voice above the noise of the mess we face. When we listen for God's voice in the mess we get out of the way for Him to move. When this happens we are able to persevere in building faith in running to Jesus before running to anyone else. We often get in our own way, which makes the waiting season take longer than it should because our stupid pride gets in the way. Pride can create unforgiveness, anger, jealousy, or insecurity. You name anything of the flesh, it gums things up. But when we go to God and ask for His help, we overcome the things of the flesh to bear more fruit of the Spirit (Galatians 5). I love how Paul lists the fruits of the spirit, beginning with love and ending with self-control. Just before self-control is gentleness.

Sometimes in life, you need gentleness before you can learn to show self-control. Gentleness is having a tenderness with people that cannot be ignored. It is a quality of being sweet and tender when people will not expect it to be given to them. It is a peaceful soft action of kindness. Let's be honest with ourselves here. We have all been there when something or someone has gotten on our last nerve, and we just want to lose control or throw a tantrum like a toddler. Yet, somehow we refrain from losing it. This is the fruit of self-control. I know from experience in helping to take care of my nephew. When he throws a tantrum or whines because he did not get his own way or is not listening to me, I have to use both the fruit of self-control and gentleness towards him. I have to use self-control to not lose it and yell at him but respond in gentleness by disciplining him with a time-out or getting on his level to explain what needs to change.

An example of the opposite is how in waiting seasons, we see all our friends or even family get what they want before we do. Then, we start throwing these "tantrums" per se, in our conversations with God asking Him why we haven't yet received what we want. Trust me I have been there and thrown these tantrums because many of my friends have gotten what I wanted and desired before me. But I have learned that responding in gentleness by blessing them instead of throwing a tantrum works better. Do not get me wrong, God can handle our honesty. He can also handle when we complain or throw a tantrum. God can handle you and your mess. Run to Him and He will help you persevere where you want to give up. In John 8, Jesus displays great gentleness towards the woman caught in adultery. The one thing that has caught my attention about this story is the man who committed the sin of adultery is never spoken of and never seen. We do not know anything about him, but what we do know is the gentleness Jesus offers to diffuse the situation and how He redeems the woman by showing her she is forgiven and to sin no more.

"They went each to his own house, but Jesus went to the Mount of Olives. Early in the morning he came again to the temple. All the people came to him, and he sat down and taught them. The Scribes and the Pharisees brought a woman who had been caught in adultery, and placing in the midst, they said to him, "Teacher, this woman has been caught in the

act of adultery. Now in the Law, Moses commanded us to stone such women, so what do you say?" This they said to test him, that they might have some charge to bring against him, Jesus bent down and wrote with his finger on the ground. And as they continued to ask him, he stood up and said to them, "Let him who is without sin among you be the first to throw a stone at her." And once more he bent down and wrote on the ground. But when they heard it, they went away one by one, beginning with the older ones, and Jesus was left alone with the woman standing before him. Jesus stood up and said to her, "Woman, where are they? Has no one condemned you? She said, "No one, Lord." And Jesus said, "Neither do I condemn you; go, and from now on sin no more."
John 7:53-8:11 ESV

In my journey, I have learned God can handle my questions. God is big enough to handle my worries and troubles. He can also handle my frustrations in the waiting seasons. He helps me to persist in my faith to keep pressing on. But I always come back to knowing God's promises are never empty. That is one huge blessing in waiting: remembering God does not go back on His word. His word and kingdom still stand. I remember having a conversation with God about how everyone I knew was getting married or having kids before me. In this conversation of prayer with God, I bluntly told Him how frustrated I was with how my time frame was running out, and how every year it didn't happen, the more impossible it appeared to me. I pretty much told God my biological clock was ticking in regard to having kids, meaning I really don't want to have kids when I hit forty but before that. God reminded me again of His faithfulness in the unfulfilled promises He spoke over me. This reminder from God was a beautiful reflection of how He helps me to be determined in faith to not give up. He showed me by listening to Him I would see how to persevere while I wait. God needed my willingness to listen to be able to see how to persevere. By not listening to God, I would get more frustrated because nothing was working out on my terms. But, God wanted me to step back, listen and let Him lead me as I waited instead of trying to do it in my own strength. The more I stepped back to listen to God, the more I began to see how my perseverance was building my faith to wait on God's timing. Even when I think He is slow, God continues to show me He is always on time. God keeps revealing to me that He does not need a watch. He gives me a glimpse of how He is fulfilling His promises by letting me know He is not slow, but is patient towards me.

The Lord is not slow to fulfill his promise as some count slowness, but is patient toward you, not wishing that any should perish, but that all should reach repentance.
2 Peter 3:9 ESV

God showed me His timing is perfect in how He has already gone before me to prepare me for the season of life I am waiting for. He revealed to me how my anxious spirit just needed to chill out because what He has for me is worth the wait. God was shifting my focus to see I must stand my ground in everything He has brought to light. I just need to wait with hope and expectation. Sometimes I get so frustrated with waiting that my anxious heart gets tied up in knots and I cannot help myself in trying to take things into my own hands. But God lovingly calms me down by awakening me again to the fact that His way is better than mine. He continues to show me how waiting is preparing me to handle the promises He has for me. That my fervent prayers are not going unanswered because He is answering them in His timing. God's unfailing love keeps reminding me He does not want me to be lost or feel lost in my waiting. Instead He wants me to draw close to Him and persevere in the waiting to hear the sweet promises He is going to fulfill.

Reflection Questions:

How are you handing over your worries to God?

What part of your mess are you holding on to? How can you give this over to God?

What does persevering mean to you?

Chapter Seven

No One Can Disqualify God's Word

Remaining grounded in our faith hammers away at false agreements we have made in believing things that disqualify God's word. While waiting for God's promise to manifest, we need to not allow people to disqualify us or cause us to doubt what God speaks over us. Do not allow other people's lack of faith to determine whether or not you believe what God said. We have to decide for ourselves who we are going to listen to and whether we are going to believe in God or not. We also must remember that each of us will have to stand before God. No one can take our place on judgment day.

This revelation of light was given to me after a discussion I had with someone about what God spoke over me regarding the relationship I was waiting for and everyone involved. Without even realizing it, this person was spreading the seed of doubt. This caused me to stop and pray for God to give me strength to not give up hope in what He spoke over me. I felt like Job in this conversation. This person wanted me to admit what God spoke over me was wrong and that I heard it wrong, that I should just curse what God said and say it was false (Job 2:9). This had my spirit unsettled because I knew what God spoke over me was true. I could relate to Job in how his friends and even his wife wanted him to deny God's faithfulness and goodness. What helped me remain grounded was my faith in knowing God does not go back on what He says. As I began to trust God more I realized nothing could ever disqualify God's Word. My faith in God has kept me determined to not waver from the truth and how the Holy Spirit leads me. God helped me keep the faith just as Job did by reminding me of his story several times while waiting to not run away from the truth. My steady faith in what God spoke to me has helped me veto the opinions of people who tell me to disqualify what God said.

Even those in our close-knit circle could be spreading the seed of doubt without realizing or recognizing it. This is where we cannot abandon what God has spoken over us. Instead, we must continue to face what God spoke and stand on His word no matter what is thrown our way. We must face our giants of disqualifying voices that are trying to get us to disbelieve God's word. This is where we step up and speak with authority over these things to see them bow before God's authority. We must speak to the mountains trying to disqualify God's word and step up with the truth and authority God has given us.

In the book of Job, at the end of chapter two, Job had to deal with this very same thing from his wife, who wanted him to curse God and die by sinning with his lips and denying God's goodness. Yet, God knew Job's heart and that he would not curse God despite Satan's temptations. It is astounding how much God knew Job and his character, knowing he would remain faithful to believe the goodness of the Lord. The enemy will use every tactic to try to tempt us from believing the truth and the goodness of God. Satan's goal is to keep us weak and immobile where we cannot reach our full potential in bringing breakthroughs for future generations through Christ Jesus. This is where the enemy tries to wound us and keep us from believing the truth.

> *So Satan went out from the presence of the LORD and struck Job with loathsome sores from the sole of his foot to the crown of his head. And he took a piece of broken pottery with which to scrape himself while he sat in the ashes. Then his wife said to him, "Do you still hold fast your integrity? Curse God and die." But he said to her, "You speak as one of the foolish women would speak. Shall we receive good from God, and shall we not receive evil?" In all this Job did not sin with his lips.*
> Job 2:7-10 ESV

If we doubt what God has spoken, then we are doubting the goodness of God. Doubt gets us flip-flopping in our faith. We can also doubt that God can do the impossible and flip situations, circumstances, and hearts back toward Him to bring Him glory. In the end, we sin with our lips and become unbelievers because we doubt or limit what God can do. We must not worry about this because we cannot measure what God will or will not do. We do not have this power to measure His ability. See, God moves and speaks in ways we cannot always predict. He is unlimited and all-powerful. God makes a way where there is no way. Besides, God keeps pursuing the coldest of hearts until they are ready to turn back to Him. But He will not force His way in. I adore how Jesus displayed His first miracle of how He moves in different ways to display the glory of the Father, in John 2, with the wedding in Cana. I also love how His mother urged Him to follow the Father's will in performing this miracle.

> *"On the third day there was a wedding at Cana in Galilee, and the mother of Jesus was there. Jesus also was invited to the wedding with his disciples. When the wine ran out, the*

mother of Jesus said to him. "They have no wine." And Jesus said to her, "Woman, what does this have to do with me? My hour has not yet come." His mother said to the servants, "Do whatever he tells you." Now there were six stone water jars there for the Jewish rites of purification, each holding twenty or thirty gallons. Jesus said to the servants, "Fill the jars with water." And they filled them up to the brim. And he said to them, "Now draw some out and take it to the master of the feast." So they took it. When the master of the feast tasted the water now become wine, and did not know where it came from (though the servants who had drawn the water knew), the master of the feast called the bridegroom and said to him, "Everyone serves the good wine first, and when the people have drunk freely, then the poor wine. But you have kept the good wine until now." This, the first of his signs, Jesus did at Cana in Galilee, and manifested his glory. And his disciples believed him."
John 2:1-11 ESV

While waiting for God's promises to come to pass, we cannot sit on the edge of our lives simply waiting for the promises we need to fill the water jars and draw water out when God asks us to. We must remain grounded in what God has spoken to us and walk by faith not by sight. It is where we have to come to a point in our relationship with God to choose to have faith or not. When we are so grounded in our faith we gain the confidence to rebuke the things that do not align in truth. This grounded faith requires the confidence to believe God will always come through for you.

Remaining Grounded

By choosing to remain grounded in the word of God and what

He has spoken to us, we are not vulnerable to allowing the enemy to disqualify what we have heard from the Lord. Also, in remaining grounded in the Word, we are not wasting our time trying to convince the unconvinced or haters who are only angry with themselves and not us. Those who are not persuaded but are trying to disqualify God speaks are not grounded in their faith. The point is, in trying to convince the unconvinced, we would be wasting breath and time trying to persuade someone who may be jealous or angry they did not hear from God as we did.

If you have not tried to convince or persuade someone who does not want to be persuaded, it is like pulling teeth or trying to lead a stubborn horse. It is unbearable. We do not have to waste time convincing anyone of what God has spoken over us. All we have to do is testify and let God do the rest. This means if we are led by the Holy Spirit to share what God has spoken over us to others, then we share it. If not, then we keep that spoken promise between God and us.

Reflecting on some of my past experiences, there was a time period between the ages of twelve to fifteen when I had this deep desire to learn how to sing. It's not about showing off or flaunting it; I have stage fright and get nervous standing up in front of a crowd of people. However, the desire to sing had more to do with learning to praise God and sharing it with others. The problem was, I had 48% conductive hearing loss in my left ear (which means I was born with it). The other problem was finding a voice teacher willing to work with me. This was the hard part. It was also very disappointing meeting voice teachers who were very harsh in telling my mother and me to meet with different teachers. They said I was wasting their time and could never learn.

Although there were many no's from different music teachers who were not the right fit for the job, God had different plans by bringing the right voice teacher and the right piano teacher to not only teach me how to sing and play the piano, but feel the music. In remaining grounded in my faith God did fulfill this desire—promise by giving me the right teachers. The amazing thing was, right after I got the hang of learning to sing with the hearing loss I was born with, God provided a miracle for me to have ear surgery on my left ear to correct it. I remember after my fifthteenth birthday, I went in for my yearly check up with the ENT and he told me it was time to do surgery. After so many years of waiting for it to be the right time, I was in shock. Learning to live with hearing loss and having to wear hearing aids was quite a journey of not allowing my pride get in the way of being embarrassed to wear them. I struggled with this as I waited for the surgery to correct my hearing loss. In waiting for this miracle, all I wanted to be was normal and to fit in with the rest of my friends. I was tired of waiting for this to happen. It was so hard being in a group of friends and not being able to hear or follow along with the group. I would get frustrated in asking people to repeat things, and sometimes I gave up and tried to follow as best I could without asking. When the day of surgery finally arrived, I recall not being nervous but having this supernatural peace that it would be successful. No one was going to persuade me that it would fail. Even before getting prepped for surgery my mom and I went into the bathroom to pray. I know, an awkward place to pray, right? But God's peace washed over me, and I was not afraid as I waited to go in for ear surgery. There was a 50/50 chance it would work. Well, it worked, and God restored my hearing through the hands of the ENT surgeon. When I awoke from surgery, I remember telling the nurse to turn down the noise because it was too loud. What I did not realize was God was preparing my heart to be ready for what came after my miracle through surgery. My waiting was a preparation to receive the gift of hearing. God blessed me with 100% restored hearing in my left ear. Going into this ear surgery I knew God would be faithful and my waiting was not wasted. This was a pivotal point in my life, going from living with a hearing loss to being able to hear. The change in hearing was swift, but it was beautiful and sweet. Waiting for the miracle was long, but the transformation was worth the wait. Through this miracle I learned God did not have to persuade me to trust Him in this, I just did.

I share this story because I could not waste my time trying to persuade the wrong teachers to work with me to learn to sing. But, I also did not have to be persuaded in trusting my ENT to do ear surgery. I trusted God with my miracle and He proved Himself trustworthy again. If I had tried to convince those teachers, they probably would have pushed me out the door sooner than I could have blinked. Their ears were not open to hearing what I had to say. It was better to keep moving until I found the right teachers, which is exactly what happened. God was leading me to the right teachers and opening doors I could not yet see. For the record, trying to convince someone with a cold heart and ears who does not listen is like running into a brick wall: you get nowhere.

We should not try to be someone else's Holy Spirit. We have to allow God to work in other people's lives from within their own hearts before their actions change, just like we have to allow God to move in our lives from within our hearts before our actions change. God changes what is in our hearts before He changes our circumstances. He has a special way of exposing our sin and the sinful nature in us so we can turn away from it and turn back towards Him to break free. This happens before we can step into the new thing He is doing or has spoken over us that He wants to fulfill in us. God changed Paul's heart before Paul changed his ways of persecuting the disciples and the church.

> *But Saul, still breathing threats and murder against the disciples of the Lord, went to the high priest and asked him for letters to the synagogues at Damascus, so that if he found any belonging to the Way, men or women, he might bring them bound to Jerusalem. Now as he went on his way, he approached Damascus and suddenly a light from heaven shone around him. And falling to the ground, he heard a voice saying to him, "Saul, Saul, why are you persecuting me?" And he said, "Who are you, Lord?" And he said, "I am Jesus, whom you are persecuting. But rise and enter the city, and you will be told what you are to do." The men who were traveling with him stood speechless, hearing the voice but seeing no one. Saul rose from the ground, and although his eyes were opened, he saw nothing. So they led him by the hand and brought him into Damascus. And for three days he was without sight, and neither ate nor drank.*
> Acts 9:1-9 ESV

Paul's objective was to disqualify what the disciples were preaching about Jesus. He was trying to discredit the work of Jesus, the Son of God. I want to point out that God dramatically flipped Paul's (who was Saul) life upside down to show him what he was doing, persecuting Christians was wrong. God met Paul on the road to Damascus to reveal to him that he was sinning with his lips. God showed up and spoke to Paul when he was called Saul and changed his heart before his circumstances changed, and later he regained his sight. In God speaking to Paul, God got his attention first so his heart could be open to receiving God's love. In my waiting, God has pricked my heart to remain firm and to not waste my time trying to convince people of what God said. I just need to share my story and allow God to change people's hearts because it's not my job to do so. This example of Paul's story shows how God can flip a heart before actions or circumstances follow the change of heart.

But the Lord said to him, "Go, for he is a chosen instrument of mine to carry my name before the Gentiles and kings and the children of Israel. For I will show him how much he must suffer for the sake of my name." So Ananias departed and entered the house. And laying his hands on him he said, "Brother Saul, the Lord Jesus who appeared to you on the road by which you came has sent me so that you may regain your sight and be filled with the Holy Spirit." And immediately something like scales fell from his eyes, and he regained his sight. Then he rose and was baptized, and taking food, he was strengthened.
Acts 9:15-19 ESV

Paul's story is an example of how God does the persuading to transform hearts. It is also about how God overturns hearts to use us as instruments for His glory. If we encounter someone like Paul before his conversion, we must set a boundary to not let the unconvinced disqualify the calling God has put on us. God has a higher authority than any man, so we should not elevate a person's opinion over God's. This is why we must not waste our time trying to convince others that God is faithful to fulfill His promises and spoken word but leave it to God to change hearts.

For instance, Noah did not waste time convincing others that God told him to build an ark in Genesis. Instead, Noah just built it while the skeptics stood around with baffled looks questioning Noah's sanity. The point is, we need to be more like Noah and follow God closely and let the opinions of others fall by the wayside. What God says is more important than what people say. This may seem blunt and straight to the point. However, it is God we answer to, not people.

No Time Wasted

Being grounded in our faith helps us to remember God does not waste our waiting journey's. He is with us every second, leading us to see that waiting prepares us for what is coming. Every minute of waiting is a divine opportunity to honor God. It also means we must remember there is no wasted time in our waiting. It all has a purpose to glorify God and to draw us closer to Him. By realizing there is no wasted time in waiting and that no one can disqualify God's Word, then we can stand on God's trustworthiness.

> *Let no one despise you for your youth, but set the believers an example in speech, in conduct, in love, in faith, in purity. Until I come, devote yourself to the public reading of scripture, to exhortation, to teaching. Do not neglect the gift you have, which was given you by prophecy when the council of elders laid their hands on you. Practice these things, immerse yourself in them, so that all may see your progress. Keep a close watch on yourself and on the teaching. Persist in this, for by so doing you will save both yourself and your hearers.*
> 1 Timothy 4:12-16 ESV

Let me clarify how we should not allow other people to disqualify us from the calling God has placed upon us: When we allow it, the door of insecurities is opened and runs rampant in our minds. We can get off track. We lose sight of what we were supposed to be focused on. We forget how our waiting

No One Can Disqualify God's Word

is not wasted. When talking with friends, we may allow their influence to persuade us into questioning what we heard from God by believing the seeds of doubt that God is wasting our time from their perspective, but they may not be where we are at in our faith compared to their own faith journey. We must stay on course, not allowing people to disqualify us or take us down the rabbit hole of doubts. When we stay focused on what is not wasted in our waiting, we see God moving pieces of the blessings He is bringing into our lives into place. Seeing how waiting is not wasted we must be persistent in being in God's presence.

In God's presence, other people's opinions do not matter to us. This is why we need to guard our hearts and minds about what God spoke by seeking God and His presence instead of looking for affirmations from a friend or the world. It comes down to having faith like Job did and not backing down from it but planting our feet in the truth. By not allowing others to disqualify God's word, we have to hold fast to how God's word is infallible and true. God's word is full of His promises—it never comes back empty.

> *...so shall my word be that goes out from my mouth; it shall not return to me empty, but it shall accomplish that which I purpose, and shall succeed in the thing for which I sent it.*
> Isaiah 55:11 ESV

This means we have the assurance that what God spoke over us will not come back void because it is going to accomplish what God said it will. His word stands true to complete what He set out to do by simply speaking it. Can you just sit with me here for a minute? God's Word is so powerful all He has to do is speak, and it will happen. Look at how God created the world, and created man and woman in His own image in Genesis 1-3.

He spoke it into being by simply saying, "Let there be light," and there was light. (Genesis 1:3). His truth is so powerful and nothing can block it from doing what it set out to accomplish. God's Word never wastes any time it will bring light where it is needed because it is the truth. In knowing God's Word is infallible, we can stand with grit on it to always remain true. When we remain firm on God's infallible Word, we can rest in knowing what He spoke over us is coming to pass. God's plan is in motion, and the words of others trying to disqualify God's word do not have to rattle us. We have the truth and God's light in us leading us in the right direction wasting no time. God began to give me strategies of knowing how to not persuade people to believe God. He does not waste any time on helping us understand waiting is preparing us. I will begin to share these strategies so you know how to use them.

Strategies:
1. Understand you cannot persuade or convince others to believe in God.
2. Recognize God will not waste any part of your waiting.
3. Seek God to know how to be firmly planted in truth to not wither away while you wait.

Identifying these strategies helped me to realize every part of waiting is a time of drawing near to God. To be in His presence and to be firmly planted in Christ. It is a time of learning to love Jesus more while you wait. As we dive deeper into waiting, we will go into more detail about how we can shut the window to insecurities and live in freedom in Christ Jesus in the next chapter. We must remember God does not waste time. He has given us a calling to fulfill as we wait, so we do not have time to waste ourselves. Remaining grounded is being firmly planted in the Word of God. Sow yourself firmly in the Word so you see nothing is wasted in your waiting. It is becoming so firmly planted in truth like an old oak tree nothing can uproot you from this place. Growing up in Michigan I learned about how my state is known for trees. Michigan is known for oak trees and maple trees, and pine trees. These trees I learned about were very old. Their roots were over a hundred years old and run deep in the ground. It also means not much can take down this old tree unless you take a chain saw to it, or if it is hit by lightning. The trees I grew up around could not be numbered. They are vast and the forests filled with these trees are colored by their beautiful green leaves. The vines and branches of these trees bear fruit of different kinds. They display the beauty God creates in nature. Each tree that is planted is a reflection of how firmly we can become planted in Christ. To get to my point, these trees are so firmly planted in the ground nothing is going to shake them. This is how we need to become grounded in truth to see how God does not waste anything. By becoming grounded in faith we abide in Christ, and by abiding in Christ, we learn Christ has made us right with Him to bear much fruit. In bearing much fruit of the Spirit we are able to see God does not waste our waiting seasons to help us learn to remain firmly planted in Him.

"I am the true vine, and my Father is the vinedresser. Every branch in me that does not bear fruit he takes away, and every branch that does bear fruit he prunes, that it may bear more fruit. Already you are clean because of the word that I have spoken to you. Abide in me, and I in you. As the branch cannot bear fruit by itself, unless it abides in the vine, neither can you, unless you abide in me. I am the vine; you are the branches. Whoever abides in me and I in him, he it is that bears much fruit, for apart from me you can do nothing.
John 15:1-5 ESV

As you see, nothing is wasted in your waiting. By being

grounded you will see God will not abandon you but take you where you need to be. Believe in God in the waiting. See Him move mountains as you wait. Allow His love to strengthen your trust in Him to believe God's word will accomplish what it is set out to do. As you draw near to God you become firmly planted in Him. Abide in Christ and you will become fiercely rooted in truth, and all you will see is God's goodness in the waiting, where nothing is unfruitful. When God prunes us in the waiting we see nothing can be worthless, because He is using it for our good. God breathes His life into us through the Holy Spirit to bear fruit while we wait. Just like God created the trees to give oxygen, He gives us breath to understand everything in waiting is preparation for His promises coming to pass. While in the waiting, we discover by abiding in Christ, we bear fruit that is fertile, and we are not to become easily swayed. Lean into the truth so you become steadfast in faith, not easily persuaded to see God's spoken words are not wasted.

Reflection Questions:

Has there been a time you allowed someone to disqualify something God said to you?

Was there a time you felt like Job did?

What does remaining grounded mean to you?

Chapter Eight

Shut the Door to Insecurities

Have you ever stumbled over insecurities?

If you are anything like me, a short, feisty woman trying not to compare herself to all these tall leggy women who have a different perspective on life. The struggle to find pants that fit in length or fit my curvy hips is a downright nightmare at times. Finding a dress to fit might be more challenging than pants. And I would be a very rich woman for every short joke I've heard if I would have charged a dollar for them. I realize every single woman on this earth has their own insecurities they have to battle because no one is immune to it.

How can we shut out insecurities? First of all, shutting the door on insecurities is a continuous process, and I am sorry to say, it is not a one-time deal. It is part of the work we do to combat insecurities. We have to expose the insecurities underneath the surface so we can find the root cause of rejection to flip them for God's truth to break free. We need the power of the Holy Spirit to work within our hearts and minds to transform us to be more like Christ. This revelation of light about shutting the door on insecurities was uncovered more to me at the Women's Light Conference in 2021. He showed me the work I needed to do to unleash warfare against the insecurities I faced. During the conference, I was on the prayer team, and the leader in charge said if anyone needed prayer before they went out and prayed for others, go do it. I literally had to arise and step out in faith to get prayed over by this sister in Christ who prayed for me to be free. The Holy Spirit led her to pray over me for the insecurity and rejection I was facing. During this time of prayer, there was a release of peace inside my body. I started ugly crying because I realized these things could no longer hold me down in fear. Every cry was letting go of the insecurity I was holding on to. My mind was renewed through prayer, and I could see the truth of who I was in Christ. God freed me from the spirit of rejection I was holding on to, knowing I am loved and not rejected. This clarity released confidence in me that could not be shaken. When this bondage lifted, I was able to pray boldly for others because Jesus set me free. I share this story to show freedom in Christ is possible. The bondage of rejection and insecurity can be broken. In my journey of waiting, I still have to draw near to God so the insecurities will not get a hold of me again. The work we do to battle against insecurities does not go unseen by God.

Fighting against insecurities is equipping yourself with the right warfare to find the root cause. Insecurities might appear in ways you have not thought of or expected before. Lack of self-confidence might be fears, doubts, or shame, and they can creep in when we least expect them. Insecurities can become a stronghold if we allow ourselves to dwell on our weaknesses or faults or the negative things we are beating ourselves up over. We need to exchange the shame and condemnation we keep hanging on to and pick up our sword of the Spirit to combat insecurities.

Shutting the door to insecurities helps us to peel away the false labels the enemy tries to stick on us. Self-doubt has this way of trying to attach itself to labels that no longer apply to who we are. They can also be attached to an irrational fear we have been holding on to for too long. These insecurities keep us locked in the past when God is calling us to walk in freedom to let go of our past insecurities. The point is, we cannot hold onto past insecurities and have freedom at the same time. We either choose to let our insecurities rule over us, or we choose to walk in freedom by releasing them. This choice is part of the work we do to fight insecurities and win the battle.

Battling Insecurities

Insecurity can try to cripple us in fear because we do not realize or see the whole truth yet. The enemy is trying to distract us with half-truths. Seeing how insecurities can cripple us because of half-truths is part of the work we do to battle against insecurity. A real example I can give is how the enemy got me to question whether God really said, "Who told you that?" by posing that question to me like he did in Genesis with Eve (Genesis 3). Satan tried to get me to question if I really did hear God correctly by twisting what God said with his question and turning it into a half-truth. As you can see, we end up basing what we know on half-truths or almost truth, and then we get so discouraged or afraid to make the next move that we stay still. This is crippling insecurity in its finest format. A very important lesson I have learned in combating Satan is asking myself this question, "Who told you that?" By doing this, I am taking away the enemy's power and turning back to God, asking for clarification.

In addition, insecurity is only the surface issue when mistrust in God's timing is the underlying issue. I have learned this while wrestling with God in this time of waiting while illuminated and basking in God's presence. Insecurity leaves us empty with no answers but full of questions and what-ifs. We will only get answers by continuing to lay our insecurity and mistrust at the feet of Jesus by going to His throne daily to pour our hearts out before Him. The answer we need to escape the crippling effect of insecurity and fear is Jesus Himself.

The Work We Do To Combat Insecurity

By continually going back to scripture to break free from the chains of insecurities, we learn to lean into God's word instead of believing our emotions or the opinions of the world and culture. In doing this, we are creating a new habit and exchanging the lie for the truth. The truth creates stability in our lives. It is something we can stand in and rely on all the time. The truth does not waver.

We see this in the first two chapters of Colossians. Paul wrote to the church about their faith and how to remain dedicated. This is what we have to do to tackle insecurity and win. We must remain steadfast in seeking the whole truth, not half-truths. He called for them to continue to be steadfast and remain firm in their faith, to not walk away or give up on Him. *The Strong's Exhaustive Concordance* gives a great definition for the Greek word *"stereoma"* of steadfastness. It tells us it is "something established, confirm[ed], and it displays stability."[8]

And you, who once were alienated and hostile in mind, doing evil deeds, he has now reconciled in his body of flesh by his death, in order to present you holy and blameless and above reproach before him, if indeed you continue in the faith, stable and steadfast, not shifting from the hope of the gospel that you heard, which has been proclaimed in all creation under

heaven, and of which I, Paul, became a minister.
Colossians 1:21-23 ESV

These words give me hope that standing firm is possible. We are able to approach God with boldness because of Christ. The words in Colossians give me hope in knowing how I am reconciled through Christ's sacrifice.

In the book of Titus, Paul gives qualifications for what makes a good elder. I shared a verse in chapter four from Titus about how holding fast to the truth is given to display how an elder must steward their faith. *Strong's Exhaustive Concordance* says the Greek word for holding fast is *"antechomai,"* which means to adhere, hold oneself to, and hold fast.[9] In Colossians, Paul shares how to stand firm and not shift from the gospel's hope. He also points out that as we continue in faith, we need to remain and abide in the truth. I just love how the truth proves itself faithful. It stands on its own and does not need our help to add anything. By shutting the door to self-doubt, we can stand and hold fast to the truth. We do not have to hold onto the past insecurities, which kept us paralyzed in fear or rejection.

We must fight against insecurity by taking what the world says and making it obedient to God's word. If we base everything on the world's or culture's opinions instead of seeking out the truth, we will become confused, distracted, and disoriented by false, foolish things. When we indulge our lack of self confidence, it distracts us and throws us into pity parties, not restoration. Basically, the world and the enemy want us to believe that God and truth are irrelevant except for the ever-changing half-truths they want us to believe or the culture of "my truth" that is shifting and inconstant. God's truth does not change and is always consistent; His word is absolute and withstands all things. We need more of the truth, not "my truth."

> *I waited patiently for the LORD; he inclined to me and heard my cry. He drew me up from the pit of destruction, out of the miry bog, and set my feet upon a rock, making my steps secure. He put a new song in my mouth, a song of praise to our God. Many will see and fear, and put their trust in the LORD.*
> Psalm 40:1-3 ESV

Shutting the door to insecurity requires a willingness to admit when we are wrong by allowing fear into our hearts. Releasing insecurity into God's hands, we have to admit we do not have the game face to win without God's help. We must accept His gift of grace to cover us in mercy. Sometimes facing our insecurities head-on means letting God fight our battles by not trying to control every little thing. It can also mean remaining in constant prayer over what God has spoken even when it seems like everyone is against us.

The Work God Does On Our Behalf

God will keep sending us reminders and confirmations of His faithfulness through scripture, through sermons, through worship, and in every which way He wants. God is not limited in anything. Even when we misstep or make mistakes, God's plan for our lives is not thwarted by our mistakes or mess-ups. Remember God is almighty. He is I Am!

When insecurities mislead us into an isolation coma and fear, we must lean into Jesus to resist it. By boldly recognizing the lies of what the root of the insecurity is, we can then allow God to uproot the insecurity. If it is caused by trauma or an open wound from the past, we need to go before Jesus to ask Him to heal the wound we are allowing to fester within our insecurities.

God is the only one who can take a heart of stone filled with insecurities and make it into soft clay to be molded into the likeness of God. We must position ourselves to hear God speak and allow Him to speak to us to let go of the insecurities we've held onto.

I have been in hard and lonely places. Sometimes I find myself almost headed back there because fear is trying to dissuade me from standing on what God spoke over me, by getting me to believe the lie that I heard God incorrectly. However, when I remain grounded in the truth, those lies fall away and disappear. I become stronger in my faith. I share this so you do not fall into the enemy's hands or his web of lies. Do not put on the yoke of slavery again once you are free. We cannot be free from sin and the slavery of death unless we choose to walk in the freedom of Christ.

Stay rooted in the Word of God. It keeps us humbly reliant on Jesus instead of our own lacking power. Here's the thing, we need the supernatural power of the Holy Spirit that Jesus gives us so we can do all things through Christ. We will not remain grounded in the truth unless we have the supernatural power of the Holy Spirit to help. Otherwise, we will be tossing and turning in double-mindedness and going from believing lie after lie without the Holy Spirit and without discernment.

In some circumstances, our insecurities can be used against us unintentionally by those around us. Seeds can be planted full of doubt, shame or condemnation. We can even be manipulated or guilted into doubting the truth, and can feel foolish for believing God in anticipation of a miracle outside our circumstances.

God is the God of the impossible. So do not let go of what God spoke. Especially if you have experienced a "But God said" moment, hold tightly to it and don't release it. God speaks with intention. The enemy speaks with distraction to disqualify what God said over us.

God is more powerful than bleak circumstances that appear impossible. God is the God of complete restoration. I love that God is more powerful than anything on this Earth, especially when it comes to my mistakes or my words that may come out wrong. The way out of our insecurity being used against us, whether unintentionally or intentionally, is by replacing the insecurity with scripture that reveals our security is in Jesus and not the opinions of others. We must remember we are here for the approval of God, not man, and we are not here to remain clouded in insecurity.

For though we walk in the flesh, we are not waging war according to the flesh. For the weapons of our warfare are not of the flesh but have divine power to destroy strongholds. We destroy arguments and every lofty opinion raised against the knowledge of God, and take every thought captive to obey Christ, being ready to punish every disobedience, when your obedience is complete.
2 Corinthians 10:3-6 ESV

To shut the door on insecurities, we need to break thought patterns that focus on fear, which cripples us in unbelief. We need to step out in boldness for Christ by finding the root-thought pattern of the problem. By stepping out in faith and believing God's spoken word over us, we gain a new understanding of who God is, by seeing how thought patterns lead us into truth or fear. By taking our thought patterns captive in prayer to Jesus, we let insecurity fall by the wayside because faith overrides fear. Faith is choosing to take courage over the bleak or uncertain circumstances set before you. God began to give me strategies for overcoming my insecurities. Here are the strategies which helped me;

Strategies:
1. Take the thought-lie captive.
2. Search scripture to replace the thought-lie.
3. Recognize thought patterns of negativity.
4. Remember God's faithfulness to identify God is for you.

All of these strategies assisted me in realizing how I needed to let go of the insecurities. Each of the strategies gave me an understanding to see my faith gives me hope to rely on God. Faith is finding hope in the unknown and trusting that God will work it out. In contrast, insecurity focuses on the problem and what may not happen or what could happen. But this is not what God wants us to focus on. God wants us to trust in Him and wait with anticipation for His movements. Faith is being aware of what God has already done and remembering how faithful He is. God wants our full attention on Him and not the circumstances or what we fear. God also wants our affection for Him because He created us for relational intimacy. He did not create us to be stuck in fear or insecurity, but for a close-knit bond with Him that cannot be broken or removed. Although insecurity, fear, guilt, and condemnation can be heavy, we do not have to carry them around.

Breaking Free From Insecurity

Here's the truth: we have freedom in Christ to break free from insecurity through the power and authority He has already given us. We just need to call on Jesus to heal us. Jesus can break people free and heal them, but we as human beings must be willing and obedient to walk through the doors that He opens for us. Otherwise, we will remain within a stronghold of fear.

> *I sought the LORD, and he answered me and delivered me from all my fears. Those who look to him are radiant, and their faces shall never be ashamed.*
> Psalm 34:4-5 ESV

We cannot free ourselves from insecurity. Our only hope is in Christ. It is Christ who frees us from all sin including insecurity. Jesus Christ is the one who breaks barriers and strongholds into pieces. Nevertheless, there will be a constant roaring battle to be equipped and put on the armor of God to stand against these insecurities and not allow them to hold us captive. Yet, we can be free from it, by calling on the name of Jesus. We must plead His blood to cover us. Then, insecurity will not hold us captive anymore. As we pray for Him to deliver us from insecurity we need to pray as though we already have victory then we will be set free. To be free from insecurity, we need to pray in the spirit prophetically over it, declaring freedom from it. We must speak bold prayers proclaiming the chains of insecurity no longer have us bound. And we must pray speaking out that we are no longer insecure but loved and accepted by Jesus. He needs to become our refuge and stronghold, not the self-doubt (Nahum 1:7). We can only find freedom from insecurity through Jesus, nothing else stacks up.

Shut the Door to Insecurities

Insecurity can be a funny thing. It can show up in different forms, just like pride. For example, insecurity can come in the form of shame from something in our past or even present that was an embarrassment. Breaking free from insecurity means we need to pray over the spirit of rejection to break free from it. In Christ, shame does not condemn (Romans 8).

The other issue with insecurity is it can creep back on us if we are not careful. When it does creep back into our hearts, we must take it to God. We have to place the insecurities back into His hands by releasing the power they have over us by recognizing why we are insecure.

There is therefore now no condemnation for those who are in Christ Jesus. For the law of the Spirit of life has set you free in Christ Jesus from the law of sin and death.
Romans 8:1-2, ESV

One sunny, spring morning just before church began, the man I was waiting for saw me in a beautiful yellow lace dress. He looked at me with a very appreciative glance, but no words were spoken between us. I felt there was no way he was thinking of me as a sister of Christ by the way he looked at me . . . It took my breath away. But then our mutual friend who is a younger girl than me walked in, and he told her she looked pretty, but still nothing was said about me. I immediately felt insecure and like I was invisible. I might as well have been a puddle of tears at that moment. Part of me wanted to run and cry in the bathroom, but I knew I had to tough it out and not break down. Has there ever been a time you've felt insecure or rejected? This story is a reflection of how I've been there before. In how I wanted to be seen in the moment over knowing I am seen by God my creator. Are there ever times when you feel confident and sure, only for it to be dimmed by the arrival or comments of someone else? Moments like that make you feel invisible, like you just want to hide or cry. However, that insecurity and jealousy we experience at times is not from Christ, and I've been in a spot where I've had to ask for God's forgiveness when my desire to be seen and valued by others is stronger than my desire to be known by Him.

In breaking free from insecurities, we need to pray for the fear of rejection to be lifted off us. Releasing the rejection to God frees us from it. Freedom from insecurities looks like creating new thought patterns.

When we release insecurities into the hands of Jesus, we are free to hope again with anticipation of what God has spoken over us. God's Word is where we find freedom in our identity in Christ, not the insecurities that have been trying to hold us captive.

Then Job answered the LORD and said: "I know that you can do all things, and that no purpose of yours can be thwarted. 'Who is this that hides counsel without knowledge?' Therefore I have uttered what I did not understand, things too wonderful for me, which I did not know. 'Hear, and I will speak; I will question you, and you make it known to me.' I had heard of you by the hearing of the ear, but now my eye sees you; therefore I despise myself, and repent in dust and ashes."
Job 42:1-6 ESV

Job's faith shows us how God's plans cannot be changed. Job believed God's timing was perfect and knew God's faithfulness. Within my journey, God had to remove the insecurities of not being enough or worthy enough to be loved, by revealing to me once again that I am loved by Him and His promises over me will be fulfilled. God showed me in Christ, I am worthy to be loved. He used Job's story to speak to me in different ways to show me how I needed to hold fast to the truth and my identity in Christ. I just had to get to the point where I believed it with all of my heart instead of half-heartedly. This was a process in the waiting season, to realize I am made beautiful in the image of God and His plan for me cannot be thwarted.

In this journey of waiting, I came to the point where I knew deep within my soul I was loved by God and not rejected. My faith became more steadfast because the spirit of rejection was not holding me in bondage any longer. I learned from Job's story to remain grounded in the truth with grit to not let go. This shift is where God took the old insecurities, removed them from my broken heart and restored it to wholeness. God took the broken, insecure woman I was and restored her to a confident woman who knows she is accepted and loved.

As I released past insecurities, I learned to see things from God's perspective instead of my limited one. God was the one who saw me as whole and made new. He is the one who created me in His image out of love. Jesus is the one who wants my affection and attention above everything else. The more I lean into Jesus to release my insecurities the more things will fall into place without forcing things to happen. When I rest in Jesus I will see Him do the work on my behalf. Laying down my insecurities before Jesus I am able to leave behind what was in the past. What is in my past does not define me, and the insecurities are no longer an entanglement but a memory. I have shut the door to insecurities and opened the door to steadfast faith firmly planted in the truth. They no longer have a hold on me. God demonstrated the work He did to free me from insecurity by letting me see how I am free.

Reflection Questions:

What insecurities are holding you back?

How can you seek and find freedom from insecurity?

What do you do to stay firmly planted in the truth?

Chapter Nine

Waiting Expectantly & Steadfastly

Waiting expectantly and steadfastly requires walking with confidence God has given us. It is an authority to walk into any room without fear. Once we shut the door to insecurities and no longer allow others to disqualify us from following God, we can wait steadfastly with expectation and complete joy. Indulging our doubts and fears will only distract us from seeing the whole truth and will keep us focused on our fleshly desires. It is important to check if what we feel aligns with what God has said instead of letting our emotions run rampant.

When we are sitting quietly in the presence of God, we can see things more clearly and the Holy Spirit can reveal more of God's wisdom to us. God's holy presence is where we can be at peace while waiting. In His presence is where we find confidence to walk with authority. It is there we can find comfort in the hope of the promise spoken over us. Healing is found in the presence of God, even healing from the open wounds and marks of insecurities.

Being still before God in His presence is where I found restorative healing to wait with anticipation by realizing God has already given me the victory. God showed me this revelation of light during my quiet time, showing me how to wait and expect the good things He brings into my life. He told me I had to stand in a posture of victory to wait with expectation. As God was sharing this revelation of light with me, I began to see I needed to shift my attention from "it was just coming" to "He had already given the promise to me." Although I have not seen the promise fulfilled yet, staying in this pivotal belief of victory is not always simple. It is far too easy to slip back into the position of being a victim and begging God to move. We must stand in a posture of triumph. God kept showing me His goodness as He was healing my brokenness. Through all the healing, Jesus was helping me to keep believing in the promises that were coming. He helped me see the difference between a position of a poverty mindset in comparison to having a mindset of royalty set in Jesus. The poverty mindset leaves us in a pit, a dark place that does not see the light of walking with confidence in Christ. Whereas a royalty mindset is a position, seeing we are no longer in the pit but seated with Christ to walk into a room with the expectation for God to move.

Waiting with expectation is connected to healing in the waiting journey. To be healed from the wounds of our past, we have to see the hope and healing–triumph God is bringing out of us. By having anticipation in the waiting, we can see more of the healing God is doing within us. Sometimes, in the process of waiting, we have to focus on what God is doing in us to see all the little things He is healing around us. When we have this attitude of anticipation while waiting, we are able to see how God is healing us from the inside out. Waiting with expectancy helps us to see we can walk with authority into any room God calls us to walk in.

Waiting with anticipation is about remaining hopeful when

things look or appear impossible. It takes diligence to stay en route when things come at us, tempting us to choose other things rather than continuing to believe what God spoke. Choosing to remain steadfast in the promises God has spoken is about believing the victory we have in Christ before we ever see it take place. We must remember that God has already gone before us and won the victory, which means we already have victory before we see the evidence of God's footprints in fulfilling the promises He spoke over us.

The sting of death is sin, and the power of sin is the law. But thanks be to God, who gives us the victory through our Lord Jesus Christ. Therefore, my beloved brothers, be steadfast, immovable, always abounding in the work of the Lord, knowing that in the Lord your labor is not in vain.
1 Corinthians 15:56-58 ESV

When God sheds light on what we are waiting for, our obedience keeps us grounded in His words until we see victory. This obedience is doing what He says without grumbling or complaining. Waiting on God to answer prayers for what is coming to pass requires trust in the victory God has already given us before the promises are fulfilled. Simply, it is believing as if the promises have already been gratified. In doing this we have the ability to wait with expectancy and we are able to stop cowering and walk into where God is calling us.

I know this is hard. I am right there with you. But let me tell you, this reward of the spoken promise coming to pass is richer and sweeter than the entire waiting process. Waiting with anticipation gives our hearts hope for what is coming. Besides, waiting with expectation is acting like God is telling the truth. It is making the daily decision to believe what God says over the circumstances. In *Renewal Theology Systematic*

Theology, J. Rodman Williams speaks of how we as Christians can persevere and remain firm in Christ, not wavering in our faith. He says,

> *"As to how this 'making firm; is to be done, Peter gives a list of qualities of character to be developed. He speaks of ways: 'Make every effort to supplement your faith with virtue…knowledge…self-control… godliness…brotherly affection…love…(1:5-7).' Faith is clearly basic. But as these qualities develop and abound, the knowledge of Christ is intensified(1:8), and they make for a confirming of one's call and election."*[10]

When we wait with expectancy from a stance of triumph, the fulfillment comes swiftly. Sometimes we have to slow down to realize it is actually here right before our eyes. While we wait, we must focus on how God is developing our character to remain firm and steadfast as we wait. In my journey of waiting, I have had to hold my tongue at times instead of blurting out all of what God has spoken to me about what I have been waiting for by using self-control. I have also had to pray in love when God has prompted me to pray without the expectation of a returned response. Praying without expectation of a response helps us to pray without fear. It helps us to pray with anticipation for what God is bringing for us and others. Praying with this expectation gives us confidence to know God is going to answer us. It is an assurance of knowing God has given you the authority to pray without cowering.

By seeking God for wisdom, I have learned waiting with steadfastness takes discernment, not to gain recognition from others but to satisfy God in every conversation I have. This means I have to allow God, who works diligently and beautifully behind the scenes, to fulfill the promises He speaks over us and to give me discernment when I need it. I will trust Him to do the rest.

In waiting with expectation, we have to walk in faith by walking in the authority God has given us, instead of cowering on the sidelines. Sitting in fear leaves us disappointed. In contrast, waiting with expectation means being awakened to the confidence God has given us. By walking in this confidence, we walk in a way of assurance, not in fear. It is being awakened to roar like a lioness without fear or hesitation. It also means carrying yourself with great boldness and confidence to walk out our God-given calling.

Stop Cowering and Walk Into The Room

There have been many times when I have cowered on the sidelines and been left with disappointment. It is like this spirit of timidity takes over my body, and I would cower in fear. There was this point where I decided to quit cowering and boldly go forth to follow hard after God with the confidence and steadfastness He was calling me to step out with. Sometimes, it was my insecurity of letting others walk all over me, and sometimes, I let rejection keep me hidden in the dark places of isolation so I would not have to face things. Neither was healthy and only left me afraid to step out in faith. I had moments when I was so afraid to walk into a room because I knew once I stepped into it, the whole atmosphere would change and shift. I felt like I needed to apologize for being there or being in the way. I remember visiting a church in Tennessee, well after the restoration of my hearing, and I was interested in being in the choir and worship team. The competition with music at this church was fierce and cut throat. The choir and worship team was large. I remember auditioning for a position on the team and being completely intimidated. The worship pastor who was running the audition told me he tried to pick a song I was not familiar with, so I would mess up. He said I had a sweet voice, but it was not what he was looking for in his choir. This memory reminds me how I let this person push me around because of my lack of confidence. God had equipped me with confidence,, and I just did not tap into it.

While in Tennessee, I met a wonderful friend who was extremely confident in who God made her. She did not apologize nor cower for walking into any room; she just did it boldly. She was confident in her beliefs and did not allow other worldviews to cloud her faith in God. My friend invited me to her small group about worldviews. This group opened my eyes to learn how other worldviews try to get us to compromise our beliefs and how they try to persuade us to cower in fear. These other worldviews try to get us to lose our confidence in who we are, when God calls us to step out in faith to walk into the room He is asking us to go. In reality, God was calling me to step out in confident faith and obedience to Him. Hearing the call of God to step forward was a risk worth taking. I came to the realization that with Jesus I have the ability to walk into any room without cowering every time. This realization was part of what impacted me to remain steadfast with expectation. The more I realized God put me in specific rooms to walk with authority anywhere for a purpose gave me the confidence to step into His calling on my life. When I was a teenager, I heard God speak over me in His still small voice within my spirit about how people will fail me but He will not. Ever since then, I have never doubted what He spoke over me that day. Because of this, God gave me strategic tactics to walk with confidence into any room.

Strategies:
1. Ask God to reveal how He wants you to walk into a room with authority.
2. Pray about where you might be lacking in confidence.
3. Seek God about how He wants you to walk boldly as a lion.

The more I began to use these helpful tactics the more I saw how God was removing my lack of confidence. He was showing me how I was finding my voice. What also helped was learning about my spiritual gifts.

Have you ever taken a spiritual gifts test before?

These kinds of spiritual gifts tests are similar to personality tests and give us an understanding of our spiritual gifts to serve God in a deeper way. I have learned recently that I am a *"feeler"* in regards to the spiritual gifts[11] test I took. In the past, I never really understood why I *"felt"* things so deeply. Now that I have taken this test, things about me make more sense. In learning this, I better understand how I connect with the emotions of God and can connect to His love for people so quickly. By gaining the discernment of how I am a *"feeler"* I now walk with more boldness of a lioness into every room. Being a *"feeler"* relates to the fear of walking into a room because as a *"feeler"* you can feel the atmosphere around you change and shift when you step into that room. Your senses of feeling the temperature of the room is heightened and your eyes are opened to what is going on around you. This relates to my past fear of walking into a room because I was afraid to feel what God was showing to me. I had to let go of my unrealistic expectations to open my heart to receive what He was teaching me in the moment. Different personality types connect with God because everyone is gifted with a different spiritual gift as referenced in (1 Corinthians 12-14). Some are *"feeler's"* like me others are *"seerer's"* *"hearer's"*, *"dreamer's"* we are all gifted with different personalities and gifts to connect with God on a deeper level to draw closer to Him. Gaining a better understanding of how I am a *"feeler"* helped me to become immovable in my faith.

Be Immovable

Rooted in faith is having this anchor that cannot be moved. This is what being immovable is all about. A faith in God that is unwavering. Being immovable is becoming aware of the confidence God has given you to walk into any room. God has been awakening this confidence in the authority He has given me to walk in freedom. You have the same access to His authority. We all have this gift available to us. Looking at all the gospels, we can see this in the New Testament. Jesus gave the disciples the authority to baptize, make disciples, cast out demons, and speak the gospel. We have it because the Holy Spirit, the spirit of Christ, lives in us. You do not have to cower in fear. You can step out in faith and into what God is calling you to.

Waiting on God with expectation–immovable faith takes more than just diligence. It takes resilience to withstand the enemy's attacks. This can come in many forms. Shame and condemnation are what the enemy tries to use against us regarding our pasts. We must be immovable in our faith to prevent the enemy's attacks. God has already won the victory by having his Son die on the cross for our sins and rise from the dead. We must position our minds to know this truth and stand on it.

Thus, to be immovable we must have faith in what we cannot see to stand firm to believe what God said. Or do we tuck our tails to run for the hills in defeat? We are called to remain in the truth with the armor of God. We need to arise in God's truth to stand with an expectation of what is to come.

Therefore take up the whole armor of God, that you may be able to withstand in the evil day, and having done all, to stand firm. Stand therefore, having fastened on the belt of truth, and having put on the breastplate of righteousness, and, as shoes for your feet, having put on the readiness given by the gospel of peace. In all circumstances take up the shield of faith, with which you can extinguish all the flaming darts of the evil one; and take the helmet of salvation, and the sword of the Spirit, which is the word of God, praying at all times in the Spirit, with all prayer and supplication. To that end, keep alert with all perseverance, making supplication for all the saints.
Ephesians 6:13-18 ESV

The armor of God helps us stand firm in the truth because we are equipping ourselves with truth and righteousness. In waiting with steadfast faith, the armor of God also helps us to withstand the schemes of the enemy and the flaming darts he flings at us. Besides, in wearing the helmet of salvation and taking up the sword of the Spirit, we are protecting the expectation God has placed in our hearts to remain firm. In knowing the truth—the sword of the Spirit—we are replacing lies with the truth to be steadfast in the expectation God has given us. The Holy Spirit will not lead us to fight a battle that is not meant for us. At times, we will fight in prayer for what God is laying on our spirits to pray over. Other times, He asks us to wait for direction from Him on how to fight. However, believing what God says and His spoken promises is our battle to fight with perseverance and grit to put the enemy's lies under our feet for good. Putting the lies of the enemy under our feet may be an ongoing battle. We learn that, in fighting the battle against lies, waiting takes faith to keep believing the truth.

Immovable Faith To Believe Quiet Confirmations

The quiet confirmation comes when we pray in the Spirit. These confirmations come to help us remain immovable in our faith so we do not waver in what we believe. A definition of a quiet confirmation for me is when God gives me one word whether from His word or a worship song or drops the one word revelation in my spirit by speaking to me in that inaudible voice of what I need to hear and receive. There can be a lyric or phrase in a song that drops heavily in my spirit to awaken the strength to remain rooted in my faith. Sometimes God asks us to do simple things that may seem insignificant when He gives us confirmations. But to God, they are instrumental in molding us into the steadfast person He is calling us to be by equipping us to be immovable. God reaffirms His promises over us through prayers or when we are taking up the sword of the Spirit. In the quiet confirmations, we are saying yes. On God's part, they are pledges of Him bringing to pass the spoken promise over us in due time.

Being equipped to be immovable through quiet confirmation is where God reveals the next thing we are to do or be reminded of. It is where God unveils what we need to see, which we were blind to before. God gives us revelation in prayer through confirmations we need to hear or see to remain firm in our faith. This is where God reminds us how He flips things for our good. It is where He brings restoration in broken relationships, in these assurances to hold onto as He awakens our sleepy hearts to stand firm with expectation. These validations are not just found in the secret place with God, but also in community with fellow believers who lead us back to standing firm on God's truth.

Quiet confirmations help us make it to the finish line with the hope to continue waiting for what is coming to pass. It gives our hearts a renewed hope to stand firm in the truth of His word. Immovable faith helps us see the glimpses of confirmation God is bringing us in the waiting. Quiet confirmations from God give us affirmation to keep believing when everything else looks bleak or seems impossible.

There is a purpose in the waiting. In waiting seasons, we learn how God is refining us to be steadfast in faith for what is next. When God refines us in the waiting, we are becoming more consecrated to expect God to fulfill His promises to us, which means we become purified through God's holy fire to become more like Christ in our steadfastness. We become more purified through His holy fire by staying committed and steadfast in God's truth by not wavering from it. By standing firm in the truth, we learn to take back the ground which the enemy tried to steal from us with his fiery darts of lies. I recently read *Christy Johnston's* new book *The Deborah Mantle*. I picked up this book and felt great anointing as I began to read it. There is something she said about the enemy that really stuck out to me:

> *"Remember, Satan cannot create,*
> *he can only mimic and imitate."*[12]

When doubts arise, we must cling tightly to God's word to become firmly planted in truth. This is where the enemy likes to attack us and get us doubting what God spoke over us. The enemy's goals are to kill, steal, and destroy. His tactics are always cunning. But our God is greater because He has already defeated Him. Knowing Jesus defeated the enemy forever helps us to be more established in God's word because we realize we have victory in Christ Jesus. This is where we need to be: deeply rooted in God, where nothing can shake our faith. It is here we need to stand in unshakable loyalty. An immovable faith keeps us in an anchored position to fend off the enemy's attacks that attempt to make us stumble.

As we dive into having a more rooted, dedicated faith in God's word, we realize how faithful and good God is. This gives us peace to stand firm in His trustworthiness. When we acknowledge God is reliable, we let our hearts come out from hiding to walk in the confidence He's given us. Sometimes before we are ready to step into the authority He's already given us, we become afraid, so we hide our hearts from God because we are wounded from past hurts that have not been completely healed yet. In the waiting, we must give ourselves permission to be vulnerable with God, so we can be healed by His love and come out of hiding. At the beginning of my waiting, I tried to hide my heart from God and other people because I allowed my woundedness to cloud my judgment. I became afraid to be vulnerable with God and by doing that my faith was shaky instead of being immovable. But God's love invaded my heart and filled the empty places, overflowing with pure love and tenderness. The more vulnerable I was with God I was able to become adamant in my faith.

Once we recognize God's trustworthiness, then we trust Him with our wounds and allow Him to show us how to be immovable in our faith. When God heals our wounds, sometimes we still see the scars that remind us how vast His unfailing love is. Sometimes the scars remind us how we got to the place of being immovable in our faith journey. These wounds help us not to leave the territory God has called us to step into but to become firm in our beliefs.

By allowing God to purify our wounds, we allow Him to strip away the unrealistic expectations that may be attached to something distracting us from becoming more immovable. Unrealistic expectations can bring hindrances and division in not just our relationship with God but in relationships with others. If we allow space for doubts to creep in, they can hinder us from becoming steadfast in our faith. The point is God is the only one who can heal us and fulfill our deepest needs by making us rooted. Nothing else can satisfy our souls like the love of Jesus. No one else can take God's place in helping us become immovable in our faith.

When Christ heals our wounds, we can stand firm in the truth from a place of wholeness. The truth is what sets us free from bondage. It is through Christ's blood that we are redeemed and healed from our open, tattered wounds. Jesus digs out the root of the wound, the lie, the sin, the unbelief, to restore us so we can walk in expectation of what He will do in fulfilling His promises. God wants us to be whole and to stand in a place of wholeness. When we stand from a place of wholeness, we become more firmly secure in our faith in God.

The reason I share this is because I used the lies of insecurities from the enemy to lead me to not believe what God had spoken. I used them as a defense mechanism to hide from becoming the woman God had called me to be: a steadfast, immovable, confident, brave woman of God.

I am not proud of these moments of doubt. Nor do I like recounting them either. But I share them so you do not follow in my footsteps. Instead, I pray you step into the authority God has given you. By walking in freedom, you can wait with expectation in the hope of what is coming. Jesus is our freedom to become unwavering in our faith.

Reflection Questions:

What healing have you experienced by being in His presence?

How steadfast is your faith?

What confirmations has God given you in your waiting season?

Chapter Ten

Waiting at the Well

Do you find it hard to believe God speaks to you with intention?

My voyage of waiting involved learning that God speaks to me with great intentionality. I never really thought about it until God shed light on how He met me at my *"well."* Yet, He did not force me to meet Him there. God waited until I was ready to find healing at the *"well"* with His "living water." Just like Jesus met the Samaritan woman at a well with great intention to save her, He waits for us, too. There are some cultural things we need to understand about this story. The Jews and Samaritans did not interact. Jewish people believed Samaritans were half-breeds and not worth being around or associating with. When Jesus met the Samaritan woman at the well, He defied all cultural Jewish customs by talking with her. But Jesus did not come to follow customs; He came to fulfill Scripture, prophecies, and the will of God the Father.

Jesus was intentional by coming to save the woman at the well just like He came to save us. Jesus is extremely deliberate in what He says to us when He meets us at our *"wells."* These might be the empty places in our hearts and the fears holding us back. Our *"wells"* can look different, and they could be a stronghold or a sin in our lives. No matter what the *"well"* looks like, God will meet us there. God met me at my *"well"* of being afraid of never being loved. This fear had been in my soul for a long time, and it ran deep. I did not think God would be able to dig it out. But He did. Little by little, God was cutting off the thought patterns connected to this fear and pruning my mind to see my worthiness and identity come from Him alone. God showed me how He is the "living water" to fill my empty *"well"* by teaching me to be obedient to His leading and to believe what He speaks. God does not rush His words or the message He has for us. He waits for us to be ready to receive it (John 4:39-42). Jesus met the woman at the well so she could encounter the truth, save her, and give her "living water." The woman's heart changed after she heard the truth by God showing her all that she had done. Then, by the word of her testimony, fellow Samaritans believed Jesus because of how He met her at the well. If the woman had run to these people before God changed her heart or experienced God's love, then her testimony would not have been as powerful, and they would not have believed Jesus was the Savior. They would not have been ready to hear this or receive it because their ears and hearts would not have been open to it. God prepares us for what He is going to speak over us.

> *Just then his disciples came back. They marveled that he was talking with a woman, but no one said "What do you seek?" or "Why are you talking with her?" So the woman left her water jar and went away into town and said to the people, "Come, see a man who told me all that I ever did. Can this be the Christ?" They went out of the town and were coming to him.*
> John 4:27-30 ESV

There are times when God lets us exercise our free will to realize we cannot do things on our own and to draw us back closer to Him. God never forces us to do something. He is patient with us, waiting for us to get to the point of realizing we need His help. God will not force His love on us. He is a gentleman. God's love is unconditional. It is simply just lavish love poured out onto us. We cannot earn God's love; we can only accept His free gift of love and salvation.

This is something I have learned more recently. When God was calling me out from believing the lies of the enemy about rejection, the enemy kept throwing these darts of lies: *you are not enough, you are not worthy, you should be ashamed, and no one could ever love you in return.* But these things were not true. Whereas God does not waver over what He speaks over us because we come from different places or classes. He also does not belittle what He speaks over us, even between men and women. God speaks to each of His children equally. God cherishes speaking over both men and women because they are made in His image. He wants to meet each one of us at the *"well"* to heal our wounds.

Jesus Speaks With Intention

Jesus meets us where we are with divine intention to make us more into His likeness. He does not shame us just like He did not shame the woman at the *"well."* Jesus corrects in love and leads us into all truth. Jesus meets us at the *"well,"* not just to show us the light but to give us the light to live inside of us. He corrected the lies I believed by replacing them with the truth, revealing how loved, worthy, righteous, and made new I was in Christ alone. Jesus had me deliberately recall all the times I was overlooked, felt unseen, and unworthy, for it to be wiped away with His "living water." In doing this, I was able to see I was not invisible but seen by my savior Jesus. He had me recount all that was ever said over me and all I had done to wipe the slate clean. God showed me at my *"well"* that I would never be thirsty again with His "living water." For instance, Jesus spoke to the woman at the well in the gospel of John with respect and integrity. Jesus spoke to her with great purpose. Everyone else overlooked, walked by, or even spit in her face because they thought she was less than. He was waiting at the well specifically for her to come. Jesus purposefully went to meet the woman at the well to free her from sin. Jesus illuminated what she needed to see to call her out of her sin so she could walk in freedom.

Jesus went there consciously to not just speak with her—He spoke truth over her. Jesus went to the well not just to share the "living water" but also to share His love and the Father's will to reveal her testimony as a witness of restoring what is broken into wholeness. Jesus did not condemn the woman at the well. Instead, He lovingly showed her who He was and who she was. He revealed that the love of the Father is available to her without condemnation. Jesus purposely showed this woman at the well that He was the Messiah and how He loved her. Jesus was also deliberate about revealing to her who He was in allowing her to be the first witness of sharing who He was with others.

This is how Jesus speaks to all of us. We just need to be willing to listen to and obey what He says. Jesus deliberately went to Sychar in Samaria to meet with this woman, and he does the same thing with us. However, we do have to seek Him to know Him and to hear what He speaks over us. God wants us all to experience His "living water," which never runs dry. See, Jesus could have taken a different route and bypassed Sychar, but Jesus went there purposefully to meet with this woman because she was a daughter of God.

A woman from Samaria came to draw water. Jesus said to her, "Give me a drink." (For his disciples had gone away into the city to buy food.) The Samaritan woman said to him, "How is it you, a Jew, ask for a drink from me, a woman of Samaria?" (For Jews have no dealings with Samaritans) Jesus answered her, "If you knew the gift of God, and who it is that is saying to you, 'Give me a drink,' you would have asked him, and he would have given you living water."
John 4:7-10 ESV

If we do not intentionally seek God and do not seek out His voice, then we are merely being influenced by this world and culture that has no moral compass. The world relies on fear frenzies to lead its decision-making process. Whereas being led by God through the Holy Spirit, we become led into all truth that does not fail. Plus, when we need reminders of how the Holy Spirit moves, Jesus gives it to us when we need it. Since God meets us with intentionality at the *"well,"* then we have to ask ourselves, "Are we seeking Him in return?" When we seek God, we will find Him. God will not keep Himself hidden from us but will reveal more of Himself so we can draw closer. The more we seek God with intentionality, we begin to see how vast His love is for us. The more God revealed to me this blueprint of how He meets at the *"well"* with intentionality, the more I was able to put it into an action plan.

Strategies:
1. God wants us to find Him and meet Him at the "well" with purpose.
2. Ask God to show you what you intentionally need to see as your "well."
3. Let the Holy Spirit lead you.

Using these blueprints gave me a fresh perspective to seek God out and learn what my *"well"* was and how I could walk in freedom. God is so gentle in removing the shame from our shoulders so we can walk in freedom. But He also wants us to know when we seek Him we will find Him every single time. God will not hide from us. He has good things in store for us in meeting God at the *"well."*

For I know the plans I have for you, declares the LORD, plans for welfare and not for evil, to give you a future and a hope. Then you will call upon me and come and pray to me, and I will hear you. You will seek me and find me, when you seek me with all your heart. I will be found by you, declares the LORD, and I will restore your fortunes and gather you from all the nations and all the places where I have driven you, declares the LORD, and I will bring you back to the place from which I sent you into exile.
Jeremiah 29:11-14 ESV

This passage in Jeremiah is a reminder that God will meet us where we are whether it is at the well or the place of exile like the Israelites, who God was restoring to them the land that they were exiled from. It is a reminder of knowing God meets us at the *"well"* to restore us to wholeness.

Jesus Meets us At The Well

There are times I am taken aback at how God meets at our "wells" without condemning us but loving us as we are. He comes and meets us and fills our souls with His "living water" to be living testimonies of His great love. In my waiting, God met me where I was at, feeling unloved and never feeling worthy to be loved. And He washed away those thoughts to show me my worth is not in man's eyes but God's alone. When

I think about how Jesus approached this woman at the well, I visualize the well being deep. It is full of water and without the ability to run dry. This well is a beacon of hope out in this desert land to keep people hydrated. Jesus is our beacon of hope in our dry lands and shines His light on the places that need to be filled by His "living water." I love how God sent His Son to do His will and meet us at the well. Jesus was obedient to do the Father's will by having a divine encounter with the woman at the well. He removed the shame and condemnation from her and called her out of her sin so she could walk in the freedom of God's love. Before she could totally be free, the woman at the well had to understand her sin was separating her from God. He opened her eyes to what He was illuminating. Jesus did not want her to remain in bondage but to walk free in the Father's love.

Jesus said to her, "Everyone who drinks of this water will be thirsty again, but whoever drinks of the water that I will give him will never be thirsty again. The water that I will give him will become in him a spring of water welling up to eternal life." The woman said to him, "Sir, give me this water, so that I will not be thirsty or have to come here to draw water."
John 4:13-15 ESV

Jesus met the woman at the well to free her from sin, removing the shame and condemnation off of her. Jesus does the exact same thing for everyone who believes He is their savior. At a conference last year, Jesus intentionally changed me by setting me free from the spirit of rejection. God did this through a woman at the conference who prayed over me. She prayed that I would know and see how loved I am by God and for the spirit of rejection to leave. I was delivered from that spirit, taking away the shame and condemnation hanging over me and showing me the truth of how I was loved in Him. God met me in a divine encounter, revealing how His love healed my old wounds of rejection. He set me free from rejection so I could share how His love can do the same for others. If you want healing, then you need to be willing to meet Jesus at the *"well"* with great determination to receive the blessing He has for you. But you also need to be willing to admit where you need help. Jesus wants to free you from the things that are binding you.

I hope you can experience Jesus in the same personal way, where He intentionally meets you at the *"well"* to free you from your own sin. Jesus can be your savior who illuminates what you need to see and hear. He can reveal or unveil what is hidden in the dark by shining His unfailing light. What I would love for you to glean from this is how God is very personal and intentional.

When Jesus meets you at the *"well,"* He will refine you in the truth to remain grounded in your faith. He is the anchor that helps us stand firm in the truth. Without Jesus, we would ride the waves of life instead of being firmly planted in the Word of God. In meeting Jesus at the *"well,"* you are choosing to open your heart back to Him, which you may have closed off from Him in the past. Even though He already knows where and when you've closed off your heart, opening it back up is realizing you need His love to fill the empty places in you. It is in the waiting seasons where God meets us with purpose to refine our hearts to reflect His light within us.

It is not lost on me how in waiting seasons, when we have been tossed by the waves, our hearts can become hardened because we have let either bitterness or offense take root in us. Bitterness and offense can make a big impact on our hearts and how we view things if we have been hurt. Wounds of offense can cause us to be blind to what is actually true. In comparison, when we are rooted in the truth of God's word, we are able to see and believe the truth. In being rooted in truth we are able to see the "living water" heals our wounds where Jesus meets us at the *"well."*

Jesus Meets Us To Fill Us With Living Water

When God removes those things in us during seasons of waiting, it can be painful because the wounds may run deep. However, the unfailing love of God goes even deeper. Jesus, who is the "living water," is the only person who revives our hearts to remember the spoken promise God gave us. He takes what is dead and resurrects us into living things. He takes our cold hearts and revives them into soft, warm hearts, becoming teachable and willing to submit to God's authority. When our hearts remain grounded in the truth, and we are willing to yield to God, we are able to see how our waiting seasons are never wasted. Waiting seasons are a time of learning more of who we are in Christ and whose we are.

There was a time when God showed me about His living water while on vacation with my parents to Sedona, AZ. The beauty there was amazing, from the Red Rocks to the Mountains. We decided to be intentional and go to the Grand Canyon while we were there. Since most of Sedona was touristy, we wanted to see the beauty in the Red Rocks and the Canyon because it took your breath away when you gazed at them. This is why we were so intentional about seeing all they had to offer. As we drove to the Grand Canyon, the elevation became higher and higher the closer we got to it. The astounding beauty of God's creation overwhelmed me. All I could do was take it in like taking in God's "living water," filling you to the depths of your soul. As we continued to hike through the canyon, I began not feeling well from the higher elevation. My dad was able to get me a drink at the gift shop to help with this sickness I was experiencing. It dawned on me this liquid was helping me heal from this illness, just as His "living water"... In how His "living water" satisfies our souls because we are filled to the brim with His love. His "living water" removes the sickness from our souls and replaces it with His love to make us whole again. He made the woman at the well whole again, and He can make you whole again.

See, Jesus will never let us go hungry or thirsty when we come to His table of truth. We get to feast at the table with Him. Let that sink into your soul. We do not have to feast on the lies of the enemy; we get to bite into the truth of God and savor it. Jesus never leaves us empty-handed when we meet Him at the *"well"* for a divine encounter. We receive His "living water" in the darkest places of our lives as we meet Jesus to worship in truth at the *"well."* Our hearts can be renewed through Jesus, the "living water," because we know Him.

The woman said to him, "Sir, I perceive that you are a prophet. Our fathers worshiped on this mountain, but you say that in Jerusalem is the place where people ought to worship." Jesus said to her, "Woman, believe me, the hour is coming when neither on this mountain nor in Jerusalem will you worship the Father. You worship what you do not know; we worship what we know, for salvation is from the jews. But the hour is coming, and is now here, when the true worshipers will worship the Father in spirit and truth, for the Father is seeking such people to worship him. God is spirit, and those who worship him must worship in spirit and truth." The woman said to him, "I know that Messiah is coming (he who is called Christ). When he comes, he will tell us all

things." Jesus said to her, "I who speak to you am he."
John 4:19-26 ESV

God, our Father, never leaves us empty but filled with His "living water," helping us never to be thirsty again for the things of this world. It gives us an everlasting joy to see we are made new in Jesus, our redeemer. The things of the world no longer appeal to us. When we are met at the *"well"* with Jesus, our "living water, " we begin to realize we are freed from our sin. In the quiet confirmations, He renews our hearts to hope and helps us to know meeting Jesus at the *"well"* is the beginning of our stories, not the end. Waiting seasons refine us and purify us. The refining process in waiting purifies us to run to Jesus instead of hiding behind our sins. As Jesus our savior purifies us at our *"wells,"* our sins are drawn out of us so we can be filled with His living water. Then, we are no longer marked by sin but marked by truth. Waiting at the *"well"* for Jesus is never wasted. In the waiting we find Jesus waiting to heal our wounds; He doesn't waste a minute of it. Meeting Him at the *"well"* we gain an abundance of blessings, moments sitting with Jesus, finding restoration in His unfailing love. Jesus, our savior, meets us there with intention, while God longs to draw us closer to Him. He draws us in to pour His love into us, filling the gaps and the dark places we keep hidden from others. God, our Father, deliberately meets us in the waiting to refine our hearts to be able to remain grounded in our faith. Jesus meets us at the well to free us from sin to walk in freedom by knowing we are no longer condemned. We are met at the well to know we are redeemed by Jesus. He lights up our path so we do not lose our way. He takes the unknown and goes before us to lead us in the right direction. Even if all the details are not there, we know we can trust Him as we worship in spirit and truth. He takes the details and works it out for our good. God works behind the scenes to work out all the specifics we cannot see in the beginning of the waiting.

Reflection questions:

What is God intentionally speaking to you?

What is your "well" where God needs to meet you?

Are you being filled with the living water?

Chapter Eleven

Illuminated & Lit Up

The journey of my waiting has been a time of learning to draw near to God by standing firm in what He has illuminated. It has challenged me to believe God for the impossible when my circumstances appear far from possible. This voyage of waiting has been a time of acquiring knowledge of how God has brought restoration into my life and shining a light on the significance of my prayers. I know God will always go before me and illuminate what I need to see and hear. The confirmations God has given me in the small things have reminded me of how good His words are. In the small obedient yeses I have given him, God has shown me that nothing is impossible for Him. Every step of my waiting journey has been about learning to believe God is restoring my life to bring Him glory. The point is God is preparing the way for us in the waiting season by speaking truth to us in love. We must be brave enough to step out in faith and into what God has illuminated for us. We must have the courage to believe God in the waiting for His restoration and the prayers He is illuminating. God shows me the way to walk by directing my steps.

Giving Up Offenses To See Restoration

Before we can fully see restoration in our waiting, we have to give up offenses in order to heal. The wounds and offenses we carry will fester if they are not resolved. God wants us whole in our waiting, not living with a wound that is not completely healed. We must lay our burdens of offenses at the feet of Jesus so He can make us whole. I want to point out that God will never tell us something bad about ourselves or about someone else. Yes, He disciplines us for and convicts us of wrongdoing, but He will never do anything to demean or belittle His children. God only speaks in truth and love. Many of us have had wounding experiences where people have shared things that were not true or even shared their false beliefs. These situations are not Christ-centered but can be driven by flesh and offense.

Whatever reason or motive is had, these experiences are not Christ-like but instead driven by the flesh and personal offense. Offense can turn into bitterness if the wound is left to fester. Wounded people lash out at others to protect themselves from being hurt before anyone else can hurt them. It is like how the Pharisees lashed out at Jesus because He came not as they expected and broke all of their laws to heal and save people. The Pharisees tried to protect their rules above lost people becoming saved. The Pharisees missed the Messiah because He did not do what they expected or wanted. They acted out of anger, and they spoke aggressively against Him.

When offense festers or when bitterness takes root, this is when division runs wild within a church or relationship and becomes unhealthy. Offense can also bring resentment, which can divide people. Division among believers is like how sin separates us from God. However, salvation through Christ removes the division. He also removes the offense in us to pour His love into us. Jesus restores what has been broken by removing the offense and replacing it with truth. I have experienced hurt from the church on several occasions at different times in my life. But the one thing God has illuminated to me in this waiting season is how the power of truth unites us through Christ. Truth brings restoration to the lies offenses have tried to tell us. He has shown me His love is greater and more powerful than anything that was said or done, and how His love covers us.

God speaks in truth, not insults. Wounded people may lash out and speak harshly, but God does not. Proverbs 15:1 (ESV) puts it this way: "A soft answer turns away wrath, but a harsh word stirs up anger." The true Word of God brings unity, so anything that causes division within the body of Christ is not from God. I am guilty of speaking out of offense or anger, and I am continually grateful for the work of rebuke and refinement that God is doing in my own heart. Jesus has restored the places in me of offense and replaced it with the truth of knowing He brings restoration of what has been lost.

Wounds can be healed and restored to wholeness if we give Jesus room to heal our hearts from the brokenness hiding in the dark places of our hearts. Through Christ the church becomes unified and restored to shine God's light to share the good news of the gospel and bring people to God. Whether it is the church as a whole or individual people, we must see we are made whole in Christ. It is through Him alone we can grasp onto restoration and let go of old wounds to heal. We do not need to hold onto the hurt, wounds, and offenses anymore. We just have to say yes to God and what He has illuminated in us. When we do this, unity is found, and the schemes of division become worthless. It is here where we find God's restoration repairs what needs to be fixed.

Illuminating Sin To See Restoration

God calls us to step out of sin, not hide our sin. God does not shame us when He illuminates the sin in our lives. Instead, He calls us out into the light to expose sin so we can walk free and in the restoration He is bringing us. We cannot live in sin and restoration at the same time. As humans, we try to make it complex, but Jesus makes it simple. The truth cannot be redefined or relabeled. It is merely the truth. People have opinions and thoughts, not their own truth. There can only be the truth which is God's Word. God is the one who gives us the truth because He is the truth. The truth is what brings people together and frees us from sin. It takes what is hidden in the dark and brings it to light, restoring what sin has broken or divided. In addition to this, God began to reveal to me how I must put down my own sin of unforgiveness and offense to see His restoration take place while I wait for His promises. The more I put these things down at the feet of Jesus, the more freedom I experience in Jesus. He makes it so simple to let go to be able to receive His restoration. Here are the strategies that helped me;

Strategies:
1. Confess your offense and unforgiveness to God.
2. Ask the Holy Spirit to show you restoration in this area.
3. Pray over the person or situation where unforgiveness was a factor.
4. Ask God to show you your sin to walk in victory.

Realizing the enemy cannot throw sins back in my face was a light bulb moment for me. Knowing I had victory over these sins was a determining factor in walking in freedom. Understanding God paid the price for them once and for all lifted the burden off my shoulders.

Sanctification And Restoration

The refinement of sanctification brings restoration to rebuild what was torn down by the enemy. Sanctification is a daily process of becoming more like Christ. It is yielding to God and allowing Him to reconstruct your mind on things above not on earthly things. Illuminated while waiting means surrendering to the work of the Holy Spirit. It means allowing the Holy Spirit to work in us through sanctification, by refining us and stripping away what is hidden within our hearts. We do this by choosing daily to surrender to Jesus and allowing sanctification to have its work in us, to make us more like Christ. We become more aligned to submit to God's authority by willingly realizing we are in need of Him as our savior, knowing we cannot do anything apart from Jesus. In doing this, we are letting His Word renew the intentions of our hearts to align with the Holy Spirit.

> *For the word of God is living and active, sharper than any two-edged sword, piercing to the division of soul and of spirit, of joints and of marrow, discerning the thoughts and intentions of the heart.*
> Hebrews 4:12-13 ESV

Healing Wounds To Be Restored

When God speaks, He speaks in love to give what we need to hear; the restoration He declares over us. He opens our eyes to be awakened to see the whole truth. God never manipulates His children to do things or leave places or churches to get what He wants. God unifies and unites churches, He does not divide them. God restores the broken people by restoring each person at a time. He always goes before us to prepare the way.

God is unity.

God brings people together, especially uniting people in churches. A church building is just a structure with walls and a roof, but people are the church. This means He brings people together by uniting them through relationships and friendships. God restores relationships that are broken and in need of healing. One of the amazing things about God is how He created us for relationships. He designed us for wholeness and mending fractured relationships that need God's love to repair them. When we fellowship, we are made greater and become one body of Christ. And when we worship together, our differences are set aside to glorify the Almighty God. When we worship together in God's holy presence, we become focused on how by being with Jesus, we are being rebuilt to wholeness. I remember sitting with God one morning when He deliberately asked me to lay down an offense I was struggling to let go of. During this time, God was asking me to let go of what this person had done by forgiving them and releasing the offense into His hands. Even though I was struggling to let go of the offense, I knew God had my best interest in mind because He loves me. I could feel the restoration God wanted me to experience, and once I forgave them, I felt a release of peace flood my heart; I was no longer burdened with the offense. Letting the offense go helped me to see how God wants us to be united, restored to wholeness, and not divided by offense or anything else.

The other thing to glean is that God does not fail us even when people fail or disappoint us. God is forever faithful. Even in our waiting periods, God will not, and does not fail us. God will pick up the pieces and repair our disappointed hearts. This is still true even when we cannot see the evidence of Him working. He works behind the scenes, and even then, Jesus can reveal what is hidden deep within our hearts that needs to be put within God's hands. When we put things into God's hands, we are yielding to Him and letting go of hidden things in order to see restoration.

God meets us in the waiting to refine us and to restore what we need to release so we can be purified. When we are purified, it is because we have been refined by God's holy fire. And we have been stripped away of the old ways of the flesh to be able to submit wholeheartedly to God's authority. Being refined reveals the grit we have to withstand to battle what comes against us. As we are cultivated by God through His holy fire, we can love others and withstand the schemes of the enemy that try to divide us.

In the seasons of waiting, God also meets us in our weakness to reveal His strength in what He illuminates before us. Being illuminated means fully surrendering to God in trust by allowing Him to unveil where we need restoration in our lives. It also means letting go of the past to grab onto the future without hesitation. Do not get me wrong, waiting is hard. It can be a long journey which may seem lonely at times. But God is always there waiting with us.

What prayers has God illuminated to you?
What do you see God restoring in your life?
What wounds has God healed you from?
What offenses is He asking you to give up?

Restoration And Illuminated Prayers

Sometimes restoration comes in unexpected places where we thought it was impossible, and there are times when God will show the restoration in us through our prayers. God has "illuminated me" to see how powerful the work of restoration can be within my own heart before any circumstances have changed. He has shown me how the restoration in my heart is key to "seeing the hope" within the promises He will fulfill. In the waiting, I learned God had to heal my wounds and offenses before He could restore the whole situation or circumstances. My heart had to see the victory before the miracle of restoration came. It is about speaking to the mountain and believing it will move because God is more powerful than any mountain we face. His love and authority moves mountains so we can see His restoration in our lives.

Everything is possible with God; nothing is off-limits for Him. We all might go through a season of dryness within the waiting season before we see what comes next. Waiting seasons do not have to stay this way. The more we dig into God's Word and pray, the more we will know Him and find Him. Diving into God's Word is where we find truth to speak over the mountains we face. Being in this deep place of truth is where we find the strength to pray bold prayers and see them illuminated by God. We will see prayers answered in the waiting, but we must pray with the authority God has given us. The more we seek God, the more we will see His divine hand in the waiting period as we are refined. In the waiting seasons, God awakens us to see new things through His eyes. It is in the waiting and refining that God brings restoration. God has done this with me by illuminating the restoration that is coming by having me pray over the situation. God is having me speak to this mountain as if I already have the victory to see this mountain moved. He often puts specific things on my heart to pray, for breakthrough and fear to be removed, and for restoration to flourish; prayer changes things. The Lord has been showing me how restoration involves receiving a double portion of His favor. God has shown me how He gives us restoration instead of shame. He has removed it all and given me a double portion of His love.

...but you shall be called the priests of the Lord; they shall speak of you as the ministers of our God; you shall eat the wealth of the nations, and in their glory you shall boast. Instead of your shame there shall be a double portion; instead of dishonor they shall rejoice in their lot; therefore in their land they shall possess a double portion; they shall have everlasting joy.
Isaiah 61:6-7 ESV

Restoration can look like little miracles, and other times they are situations of impossibility flipped into the possible, whether through prayer or people speaking truth into us. The moment we stop believing God can or will do something to restore a situation is the moment we allow unbelief to rob us of knowing how powerful God is. Unbelief can be very effective to dissuade us from seeing restoration fulfilled. This doubt and unbelief can steal the joy of seeing these illuminated prayers God will answer. But when we humble ourselves in the refining process and pray, God has this way of turning everything we thought was impossible and making it possible. How God restores things may not be how we expect them to look or come out the way we want them to. Yet, when God restores, He does not do anything halfway but to full completion. Before the complete restoration has taken place, I have to trust God that the unfulfilled promises I am waiting for are still coming. I believe and have faith, just like Job, to remain firm in the truth. Through the leading of the Holy Spirit and prayer, God has illuminated me to see the blessings of waiting and how God restores abundantly more than what we could imagine. When God restores, He goes above and beyond our expectations. He blows us away.

> *And the LORD restored the fortunes of Job, when he had prayed for his friends. And the LORD gave Job twice as much as he had before.*
> Job 42:10 ESV

Seeing restoration take place through prayers is an unfolding of God's refinement through purification. Let me be honest, in the refining process, before the restoration of healing has taken place, our hearts have to be in a position of humility to receive. Besides, before any healing can take place, there needs to be time for God to prepare the other people involved. The hard part of waiting is realizing restoration takes time. We have to pray bold prayers for the people around us and renew our hearts to keep believing for what is to come while waiting. Remember, God is working through it all, even behind the scenes, to fulfill what needs to be restored.

> *The LORD is my shepherd; I shall not want. He makes me lie down in green pastures. He leads me beside still waters. He restores my soul. He leads me in paths of righteousness for his name's sake.*
> Psalm 23:1-3 ESV

Illuminated prayers are having the peace of knowing God is bringing the answer. It is not questioning God's timing but trusting He is always on time.

Unforgiveness And Restoration

Seeing restoration take place is the key to forgiveness. We cannot hold onto unforgiveness and expect God to bring us restoration. Forgiveness, healing, and restoration are all tied together. During the waiting season, after all the things we do not need are stripped away, the only thing left is to allow God to heal the wounded places in our hearts so restoration can be fulfilled.

Restoration cannot happen if we are gripping too tightly to unforgiveness or not allowing God to heal our hearts. Forgiveness brings healing into our hearts, and healing allows restoration to occur by preventing bitterness from taking root, letting love flow through us. God has illuminated me to see I could not hold on to unforgiveness and grab ahold of restoration. He would not allow me to hold tightly to things I needed to let go of. He used a great friend to speak into my life, helping me to count up the debt of unforgiveness, wounds, and offenses so I could walk in the restoration God was calling me to. After doing this exercise several times during my prayer time, a peace washed over me like none I'd ever experienced. I let go of the unforgiveness and gained peace to restore my soul. This peace washed over me and let me rest in God's grace, knowing He was comforting me when I needed it. Sometimes God's peace surprises me with how swiftly it comes and how quietly it can give my soul rest.

Refined And Illuminated Prayers

In the waiting is where God refines us to become more like Him. This is where God can dig deep into hearts to draw out of us what needs to be illuminated. Sometimes in the waiting season, God strips away the unbelief we have been holding onto. When there is unbelief in our hearts, we stop believing what God says and start believing the enemy's lies. This is when we need God to illuminate prayers so we can be aware of what He is refining in us; to be conscious of what God is restoring in us to let go of unbelief. The more we believe and act like God is telling us the truth the more our hearts will be renewed with hope to expect God's blessings. This is when God has to tear down those high places in our lives to uproot the lies.

When the high places of strongholds do come down, it is like a flood of peace in our hearts. With complete transparency, the waiting season can be the hardest season we go through. It is a pruning season where we are refined by God. This season of waiting can be exhausting, but it can be the most rewarding. As we dig deeper with God in the truth, we get a clear picture of how faithful He is. As God polishes us in the waiting, we grow deeper in Christ, praying with authority and believing the illuminated prayers God has put in our hearts. Waiting requires being willing to submit to God, which cultivates us in our waiting season. When we are refined by God, we get an intimate relationship with Him and can see how good His character is. The more we are refined, the more we are able to see how God never loses a battle because He is setting us apart to see new things. Waiting can be fulfilling because God shows us how His word draws us closer to Him as we are being purified.

From the fruit of a man's mouth his stomach is satisfied; he is satisfied by the yield of his lips. Death and life are in the power of the tongue, and those who love it will eat its fruits.
Proverbs 18: 20-21 ESV

As we are purified and refined by God, our patience is tested to wait on the Lord. I have learned a great deal about my refined prayers. God has shown me the power of my words in how they can bring life or death. My words can bring life and speak of

His restoration over my situation, or if I speak negatively, I can speak death and expect a different outcome. When I approach things with a hopeful attitude, I know He is my provider and His answer brings peace and not worry. I know with God, I do not have to worry or be afraid. In my life, I have faced some medical situations full of unknowns and waiting. By being faithful and trusting in Him, I have experienced Him bringing the right doctor in my path to help find answers; a doctor who truly cares and wants me to get better, and wants to help find a solution. Ultimately, I know God is my healer and He will restore me, even in the waiting. Although my faith has been tested while waiting on God in my circumstances, it has helped me remember God is my resource and restorer. Despite facing difficult and unknown things, I can keep my hope in Jesus. I must continue to speak life over them, and in this, God will illuminate these prayers I have prayed. They will give me hope to keep going. I can rest and know Jesus is the one who helps me pick up my lantern and leads me in the light while I wait.

Waiting seasons look different for different people. God calls us to believe what He speaks over us in waiting as He purifies our minds. He takes the old thoughts and wipes them away to give us a clean slate. The Lord does this through transforming our hearts. God refines us by removing the impurities to leave us without blemishes. When we sit with God to meditate on His word, we are being renewed to see that He has shifted our hearts to see things more clearly. He takes our prayers and casts light on what we need to pivot in speaking life over death in our prayer lives. These prayers illuminate the power in our words, in breaking chains, healing, and clarity. Our Lord Jesus will shine a light on our prayer lives to see them more clearly when He shows us the freedom they can bring. Through our prayers, God is purifying our hearts and lips to speak out the refinement He is doing in us. Refinement is a process of going through fire without getting burned. It is the same when gold is being refined through fire; it becomes soft and forms into a liquid state so the impurities come to the top and can be removed. The impurities are being removed from the gold; no matter how hot it gets, it will not get burned. It is the same for us. The more God refines us, the more impurities are removed. We just need to be obedient to what God asks us to do. Then He can use our obedience in waiting to encourage others in their own waiting, becoming more refined through fire without getting burned.

Revelations Of My Lantern Story

Let me encourage you, waiting is a time of grasping how God gives us light when we feel lost in our voyages of waiting. God can give us visions and dreams with light to convey things we need to learn while we wait. These can be a reflection of God giving us revelations to discover His love in a new way. My hope is that you are open to seeing what God shows in your waiting. Walking with God in anticipation without losing hope takes tenacity and audacity. Seasons of waiting will test our faith and whether or not we believe God. This time of waiting will also unveil how well we wait, in what God reveals things we need to see. In the waiting, we will be illuminated by Him and tested in our obedience to being refined. This waiting and refining process are times of eye-opening revelations of if we believe what God says or not; in dreams, His Word, and worship, they will be filled with choices to believe or let doubt rule inside of your heart.

Each of us will have to decide whether to accept God's revelations or choose unbelief. These are just simple facts that I have faced in my journey of waiting. By choosing to walk in light, God illuminates my every step. This is the same for you. God is with you always, leading you into the light, unveiling to you the next thing you need to grab ahold of. Sometimes His revelations of light are subtle, and sometimes, they are completely obvious. It is your choice to search it out and draw near to Him. You will be faced with seeing God's Word as a lamp to your feet and a choice to pick up your lantern and follow Him.

Your word is a lamp to my feet and a light to my path.
Psalm 119:105 ESV

One night before God put it on my heart to write this book, I dreamed of walking along the beach at night with a lantern in my hand. As I walked, I knew God was leading me through each step, even though I could not see Him. In this dream, I kept walking, and with each step I took, God used the lantern to light the next step I was to take. The further I continued, the closer I came to the edge of the beach, where it was met with tall oak trees. As God led me to take the last step to the trees, he had me sit under them in the quiet to worship Him with praise and song. He prepared my heart to trust Him in the unknown and for the next step to take. He lit my path with a lantern to display light.

This dream was an unveiling to how He will always be my faithful guide, never leaving my side in the waiting. It is a reflection of my waiting journey in trusting God with each step I take and how He has illuminated what is before me, what is behind me, and what He has prepared me to step into. It is also a reflection of how His Word is a lamp to my feet so I will not stumble but take a position that is lit up before me. The dream helped me see that I do not have to know everything but can rely on God to illuminate what is next and trust He has my back. It prepared me for what God was calling me to write and share with others. Even though I could not realize where I would end up, I knew I could trust Him to lead me in the right direction. It was also preparing me to be ready for what God was asking me to step out in faith to believe without having all the details. God was preparing me to pick up my lantern to follow Him in the waiting to see an adventure filled with abundant blessings lit by His love.

Illuminated Lanterns

I love how God used the lantern story to influence my trust and belief in Him. God used this dream and vision to help me remember how getting closer to Him in this waiting is filled with abundant joy. Within our adventurous journeys of waiting, God is illuminating what we need to believe by giving us the understanding to know what to do. He is challenging our faith to grow by giving us more faith to believe in what we do not see but have hope for. God is opening the door for us to see His provision in waiting. I have learned God is providing for me in the waiting through the promises He is fulfilling. He is leading me by His Word, giving light to where I need it so I do not become lost. The Lord has taught me He is trustworthy in my waiting, and every mountain I face, He will move, so I can walk right through it guided by the lantern of His light. God will do the same for you. You just have to ask Him.

In this journey of waiting and being illuminated by God, we learn to dig deep within our faith to know God more and understand who He is. We also learn more about who we are in Christ, so we can believe what God is speaking to us. God gives us the opportunity to pick up our lanterns in waiting to go deeper with Him. God teaches us how to listen for His voice above all the noise of this world and culture. Above all, God shows His faithfulness in the waiting by never failing to keep His promises and by giving us confirmation throughout the journey, giving us hope to understand the purpose of waiting.

The unfolding of your words gives light; it imparts understanding to the simple.
Psalm 119:130 ESV

Waiting with God and being illuminated is a time of refinement by arising in the light God has given us. He puts the lanterns in our hands to seek out His love in every part of our lives while we wait. The more we lean into seeking God out the more the lanterns in our hands grow brighter. In learning more about who God has called you to be, you can step out with the confidence and authority He has already given you. My story of waiting may seem open-ended. However, deep within my bones, deep within my soul, I know the waiting season is coming to a close. The breakthrough is coming swiftly like the dawn morning sunlight. It will be a whirlwind, but it will also be sweet. Just like the soft rain on a spring day. My waiting is filled with God's bright light shining down on me. It is bright, like an aisle lit with lanterns leading to meeting my bridegroom at the end. It is Jesus Himself, my abundant love. He is the one worth the wait.

How do I know for sure the waiting is coming to a close? The answer is God is faithful, and deep within my spirit, I know a breakthrough is coming. May this lantern story be a revelation for you to see God is leading you while you wait. Let the lantern of hope in your hand, God's Word, burn bright to shine its light on your journey of waiting. I hope it is a time you learn to draw near to Jesus and allow Him to light your path with His Word. I realize to you, as the reader, it may seem crazy to say and declare these things. God has illuminated to me to keep the faith, standing firm because what He has spoken over me has been confirmed in His Word, in prayer, and in people around me whom I trust. Although this deep conviction in my spirit gives me faith to continue to stand firm, I know my God is making a way, and I know His Word proves true.

> *For it is you who light my lamp; the LORD my God lightens my darkness. For by you I can run against a troop, and by my God I can leap over a wall. This God—his way is perfect; the word of the LORD proves true; he is a shield for all those who take refuge in him.*
> Psalm 18:28-30 ESV

May you have the courage to take God at His Word and believe it. And I hope you believe God speaks to you with wonderful promises. Believing God over the circumstances is half the battle of seeing breakthroughs around the corner. I pray you have the faith to believe in God, foolish faith to follow Him even if you have to wait for a while, He will be your refuge, a lamp unto your feet. Allow yourself to dig deeper with God and know He guides you in each step and every turn.

> *And your ears shall hear a word behind you, saying, " This is the way, walk in it," when you turn to the right or when you turn to the left.*
> Isaiah 30:21 ESV

Believing and declaring the truth is part of the battle. Speaking the truth is where we may look foolish to the world and those who do not understand. This is where my faith comes in, backing up my belief and convictions to remain steadfast to the truth. If I do not remain in constant faith, then I will be tossed around like the waves in the ocean. My journey of waiting is coming to an end even if I do not see it just yet. Deep within my soul, I know my God is faithful so my heart can rest in His unfailing love. I can rest in Jesus and know He is guiding me with His light through my waiting and will never leave me.

My ambition for sharing my story of waiting is to be a beacon of hope for you, a light in the darkness to show you are not alone in your waiting. God put this story on my heart so others could see nothing is wasted in the waiting and God is trustworthy. In this journey, learning to trust God to release things into His hands is a process of refinement. I anticipate you can see your waiting is coming to an end. I hope you can see the banner of hope God has placed on your heart to remain steadfast in faith. Do not allow the frustrations in waiting to distract you from seeing what God is doing in your life. Focus your mind on the lantern God is placing in your hands to walk in His light.

Moreover, I have learned that controlling everything gets you nothing but frustration. In comparison, putting things back into God's hands takes the burden off of me. I should have never tried to take control in the first place. However, the refinement has been filled with lovely moments with Jesus sweetly speaking over me to quiet my soul and draw me closer to Him, remaining firm in holding fast to the truth and His promise over me. I hope and pray this book draws you closer to Jesus to believe His every word. Nothing is sweeter than God's spoken promises being poured out on you. He is lavish with His words and love. I hope you receive it with open arms and a warm soft heart. The outpouring of God's promises helps us to stand firm by the truth He speaks over us.

I urge you to press into the presence of God when frustrations try to entangle you in lies. Let God's presence fill you and illuminate you to see His love drawing you near to Him. By pressing into God's presence, you will be renewed to stand firm in faith with the grit to be immovable. May God's unfolding words light your path to stay the course of what He is calling you to wait for. You are God's light, so let that light arise from within and overflow into the lives of others. I pray His light illuminates every step you take so you can walk in the truth to not stumble, remaining steadfast in the light. I am laying before you a call of action to keep sitting in God's presence and believe His promises. It is God's light within you that breaks the strongholds of fear. I pray God's spoken word over you lights the way to walk in truth with confident boldness. God is still writing your story and is revealing His light more and more. Allow God's Word to be a lantern in your journey of waiting to guide you in every step you take.

Arise and walk in the promises of God. Throw off your fear and shame to run to Jesus!

Arise, shine, for your light has come, and the glory of the LORD has risen upon you.
Isaiah 60:1 ESV

Reflection Questions:

What understanding has God revealed to you in waiting?

What different kinds of revelations has God given you?

Have you been able to let go of unforgiveness in your own heart?

What restoration have you experienced or hoped for in your waiting season?

Notes

1. Apple Dictionary, Copyright © 2005–2019 Apple Inc. All rights reserved.

2. The Holy Bible English Standard Version, Crossway Publishing, Wheaton IL, 2001,

3. Cunnington, Havilah, Truth to Table Prophetic Personalities Test, https://truthtotable.com/feeler-personality/ (Accessed, April 8th, 2023).

4. Goll, W. James, The Discerner, Hearing, Confirming, And Acting on Prophetic Revelation Whiter House Publishers, New Kensington PA, 2017

5. Johnston, Christy, The Deborah Mantle, A Woman's Call To Arise And Slay The Giants Of her Generation, Destiny Image, Shippensburg PA, 2023

6. MacAuthor, John, The MacAuthor Bible Commentary, Unleashing God's Truth, One Verse At A Time, Nashville TN, Thomas Nelson, 2005

7. MacDonald, William. Believer's Bible Commentary, A Complete Bible Commentary In One Volume, Nashville

TN, Thomas Nelson, 1995

8. Robert Morris, Finding Purpose in Waiting: Trusting God's Perfect Timing, https://www.youtube.com/watch?v=TNZwPePRbxU Accessed (February 6, 2024)

9. Rollin, Jason, City Light Church, Detroit Michigan, In Between the Pain and the Promise, https://citylightchurch.com/ondemand Accessed (April 8th, 2023).

10. Strong, James, LL.D, S. T. D., The New Strong's Exhaustive Concordance Of The Bible, Nashville TN, Thomas Nelson, 1990

11. Williams, J. Rodman, Renewal Theology Systematic Theology from a Charismatic Perspective, Grand Rapids, Michigan, Zondervan, 1992

Acknowledgements

Mom & Dad, Thank you for encouraging me to follow my dreams and God's leading. Both of you have been my rock and support system through everything. I love you beyond what words can even describe.

Taylor Phillips, I could not have gotten here without you! You are a blessing and strength like none other. Your encouragement and words of affirmation are dear to my heart. Sis, You have talked me through so much and maybe even did not realize it. Girl, you have helped me keep my confidence in times I have wanted to give up. Thank you for your words of fire. Tay, your heart and fire for God has lit a fire in me to believe in the impossible. All I can say is thank you for telling me to write this book.

Ashley Ferris, Thank you for making me laugh and guiding me through everything. Thank you for praying for me and for always being so sweet. Friend, I could not have done this without you. Thank you for coaching me and listening to all my thoughts and ideas when they were just a scrambled mess. You are an amazing coach and friend.

Amber Olafsson, Thank you for always having my back and for seeing things in me that I have never seen before. Thank you for calling things out within me that God placed there, but I was too afraid to see or even believe. Girl, you have blessed me because you are a blessing.

Jessica Russell, Thank you for your feisty-sassiness which keeps me in check and for praying over me when I need it. Your friendship means the world to me.

UHP Team You are miracle workers and beyond amazing. Thank you for helping me become a better writer. The revision team is fantastic. Thank you for helping me make more sense and making me sound better.

Tommy & Cheryl McCaul, Thank you for allowing me to learn how to lead and learn what ministry looks like. Thank you for mentoring and challenging me in college through youth ministry to be a vessel for God to use. Thank you for allowing God to speak to me through you guys. Thank you for calling things out within me. Thank you for teaching me what saying yes to God looks like. I have learned so many things from both of you. Thank you for your willingness to serve God with all of your hearts. Most of all, thank you for being a mentor and friend.

About the Author

Elizabeth loves Jesus and her family. She is a graduate of Grace Bible College (Grace Christian University) with a Bachelor's degree in Leadership & Ministry. Elizabeth loves going to the beach and soaking up the sun in her hometown in Michigan. She enjoys working with youth and young adult ministries within her community as well as spending time with her friends playing volleyball, softball, and golf. You can find her curled up in a comfy chair with a cup of strong coffee, writing and blogging about connecting with Jesus. Elizabeth has a spiritual fire to speak encouragement and is excited to help women break free from insecurity to live free. She also enjoys helping others bring their kingdom messages to life. As a believer, she enjoys helping women know who they are in Christ by believing the promises of God which you will be able to read about in her debut book "Illuminated While Waiting". She loves to illuminate Jesus on her blog at: https://gypsygirlhughes9.wixsite.com/illuminatedandlitup

www.ingramcontent.com/pod-product-compliance
Lightning Source LLC
Chambersburg PA
CBHW070056080526
44586CB00013B/1080